Table of Contents

LEVEL B

Unit 1

Unit 2

Unit 3

Unit 4

Table of Contents

LEVEL B

Here's what to do!

Say the name of each picture. Print the capital and small letters for its beginning sound.

1
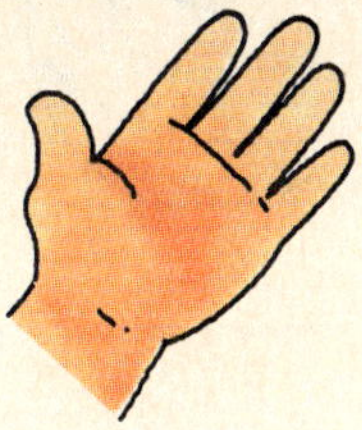

2

3

4

5

6
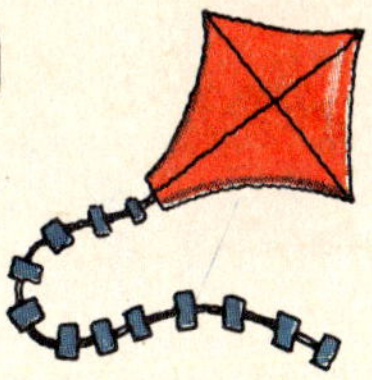

7

8
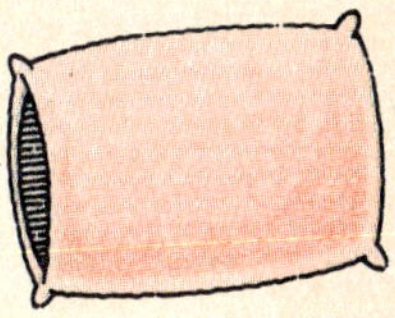

9

10

11

12

13
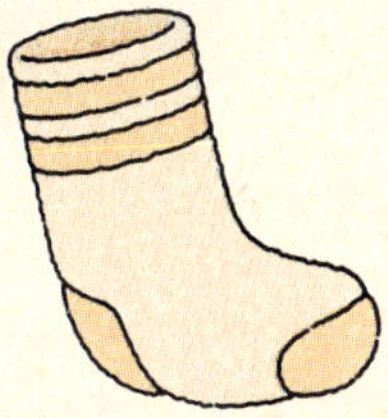

14
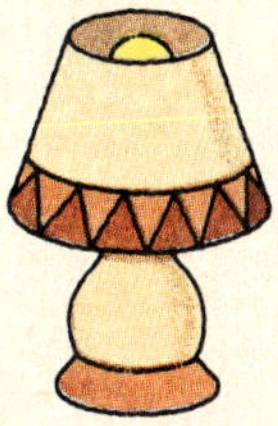

15

16

Here's what to do!

Say the name of each picture. Print the letter for its beginning sound. Trace the whole word.

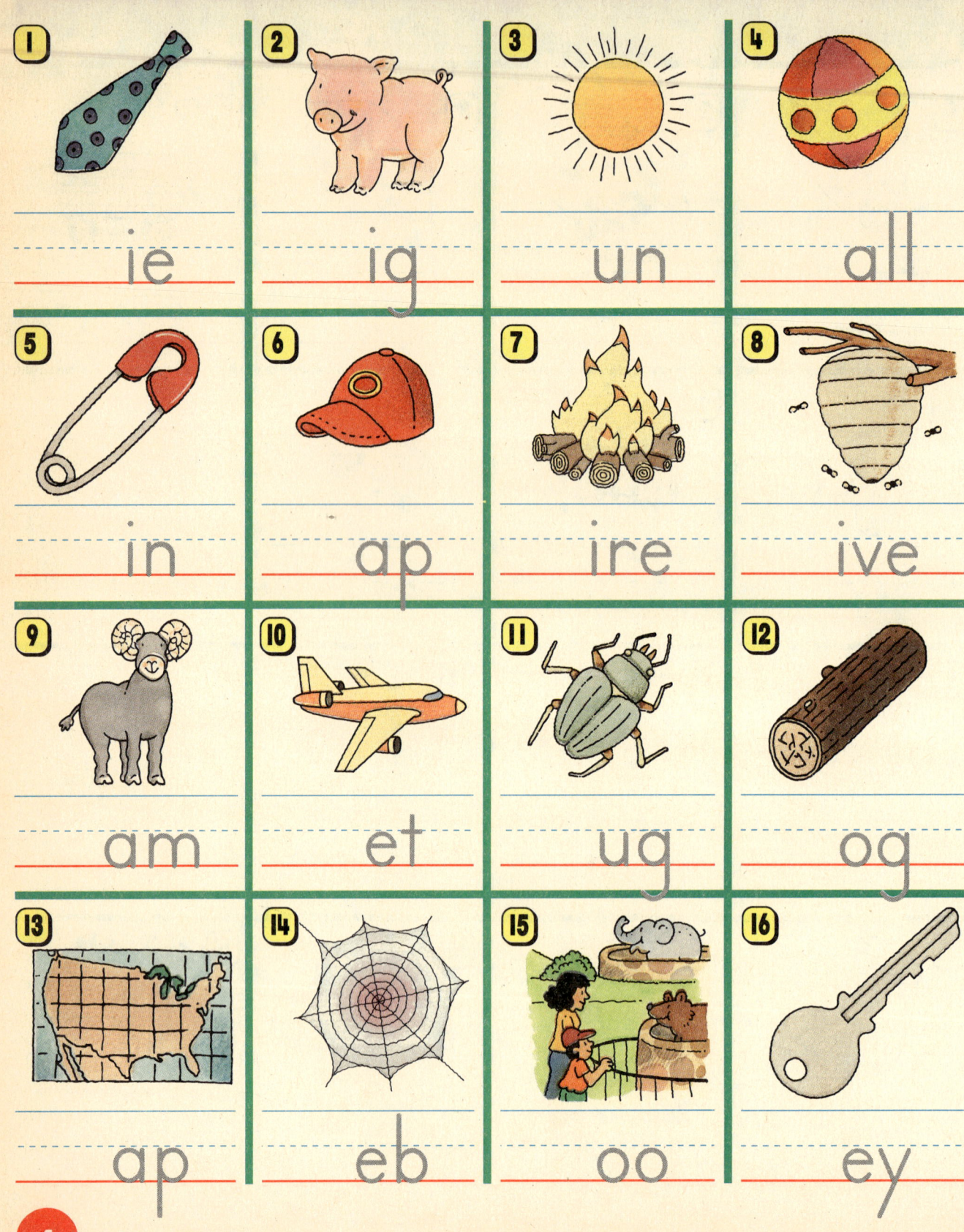

1

___ie

2

___ig

3

___un

4

___all

5

___in

6

___ap

7

___ire

8

___ive

9

___am

10
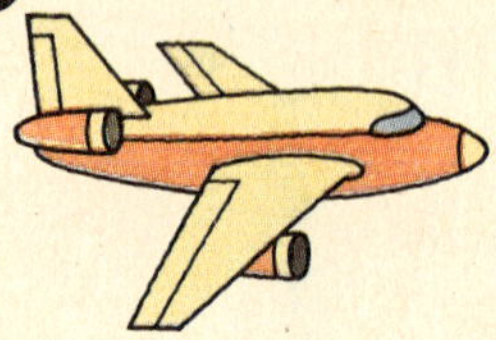
___et

11

___ug

12

___og

13
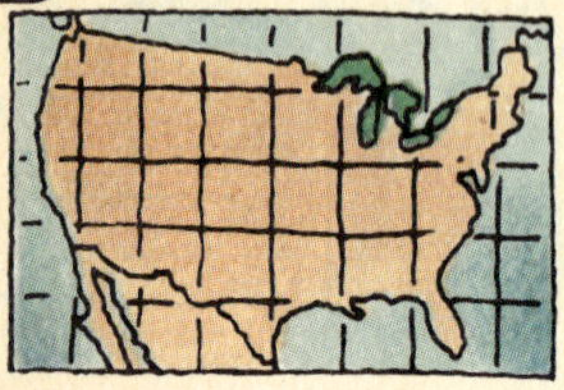
___ap

14
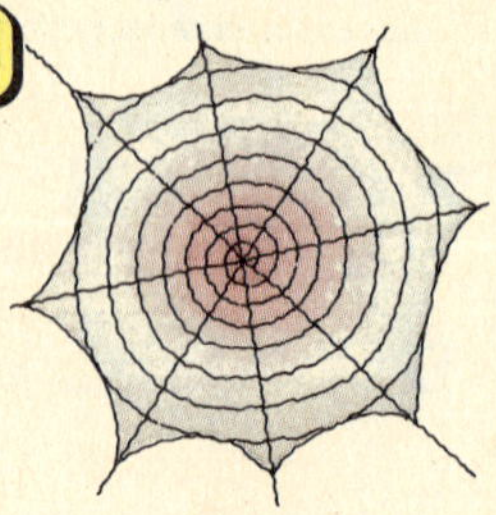
___eb

15

___oo

16

___ey

Here's what to do!

Say the name of each picture. Print the letter for its ending sound. Trace the whole word.

1 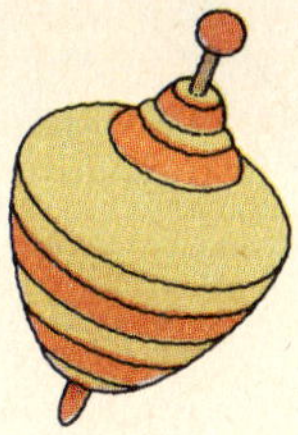
to

2 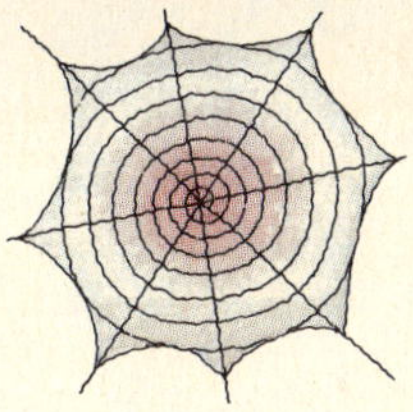
we

3 
do

4 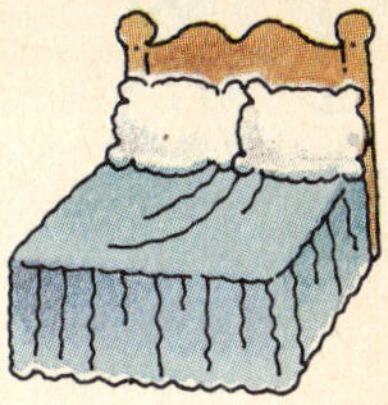
be

5 
tai

6 
cu

7 
su

8 
bu

9 
ha

10 
lea

11 
bo

12 
dru

13 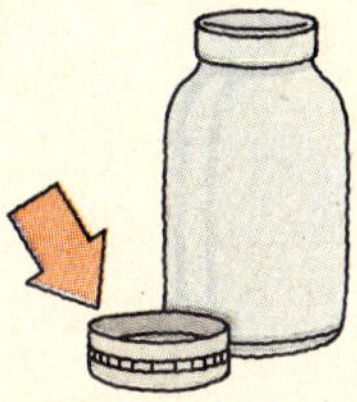
li

14 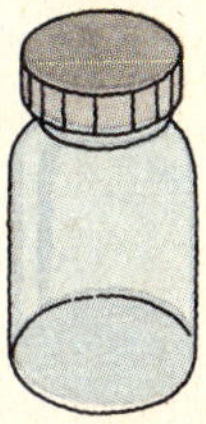
ja

15 
bir

16 
bow

Here's what to do!

Say the name of each picture. Print the letter for its ending sound.

1

2

3

4
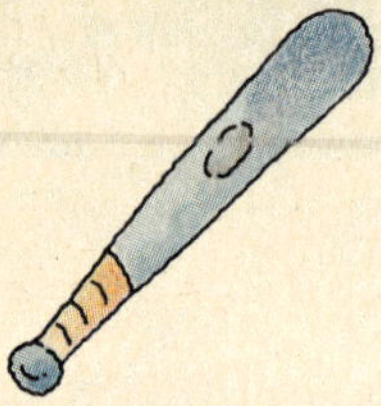

5

6

7

8

9

10

11

12

13

14

15
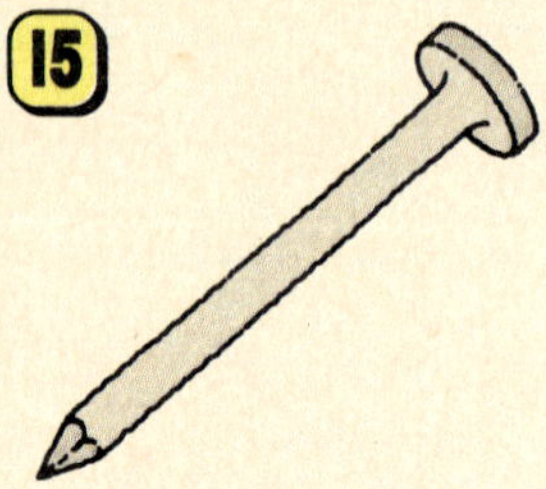

16
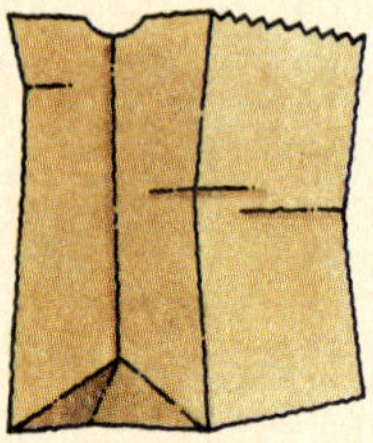

Now try this!

Look at the letters and the picture in each box. Say the name of the picture. If you hear the sound of the letter at the beginning, circle the letter on the left. If you hear the sound at the end, circle the letter on the right.

1 s  s	2 d 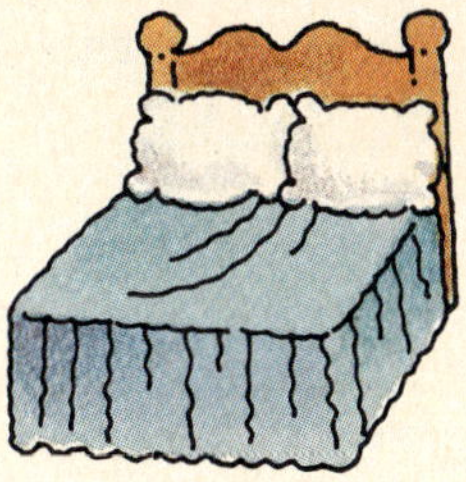 d	3 g  g
4 h  h	5 f  f	6 p 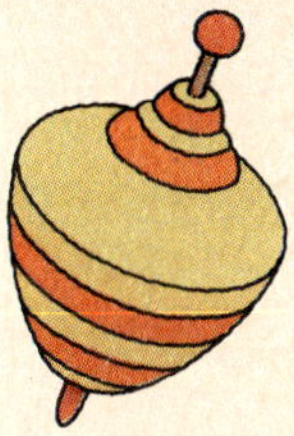 p
7 r  r	8 m 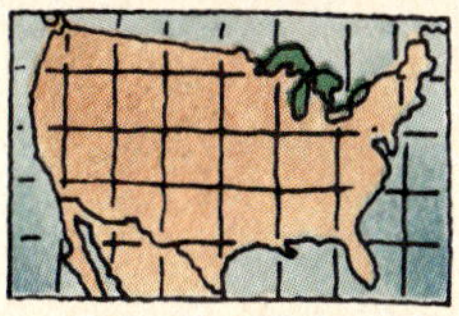 m	9 k  k
10 y  y	11 t  t	12 j  j
13 w 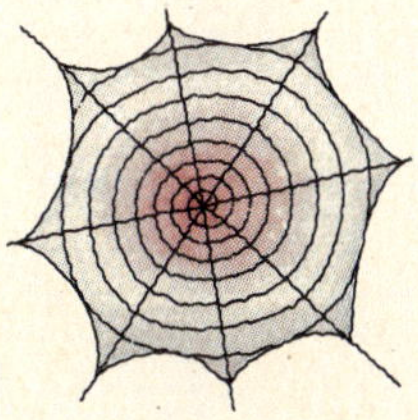 w	14 b  b	15 n  n

Here's what to do!

Say the name of each picture. Print the letter for its beginning sound. Then print the letter for its ending sound. Trace the whole word.

1

o

2

a

3

u

4

e

5

u

6

o

7

i

8

a

9
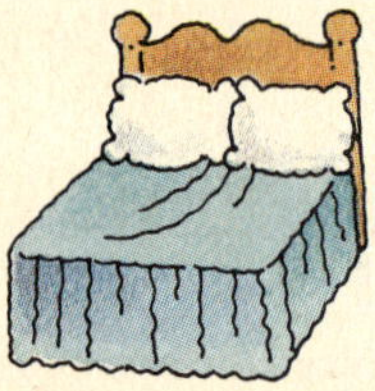
e

10
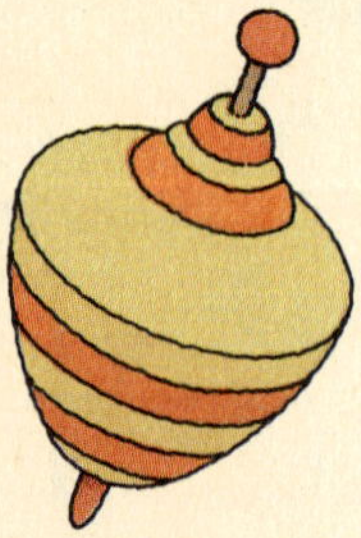
o

11
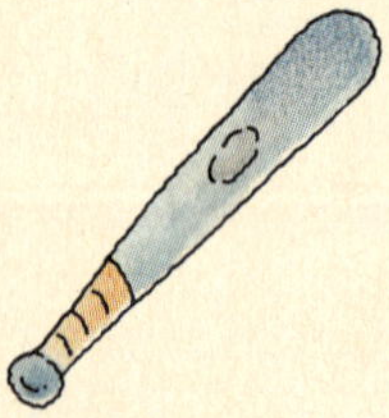
a

12

e

Here's what to do!

Say the name of each picture. Print the letter for its middle sound.

1
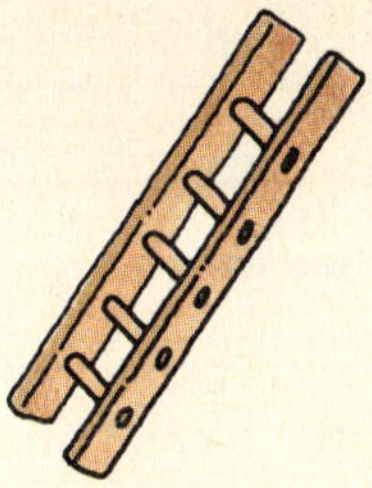
d

2

3

4
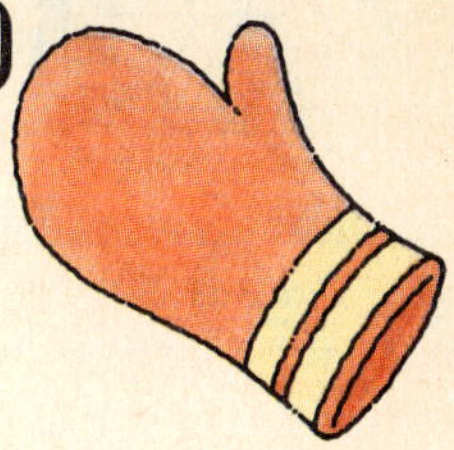

5

6
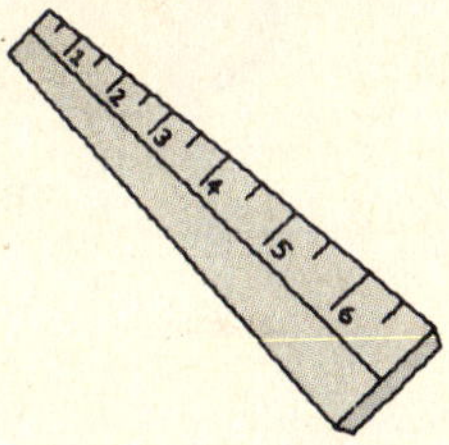

7

8

9
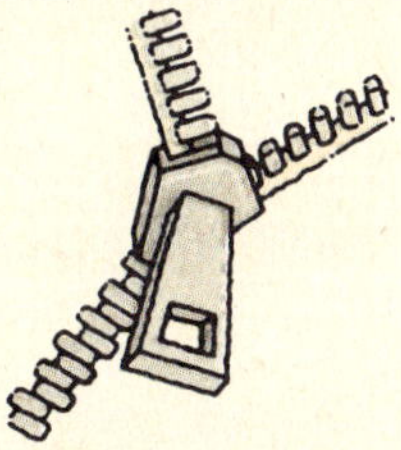

10

11

12

13

14
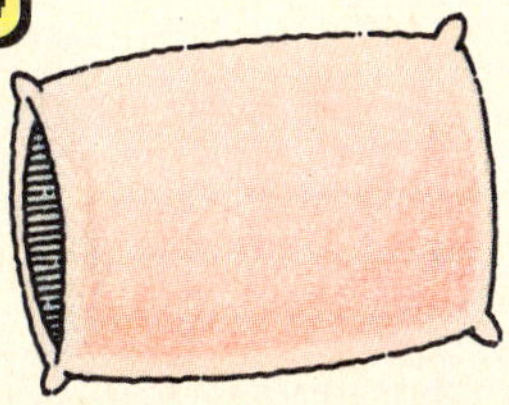

15

16

Here's what to do!

Say the name of each picture. Print the letter for its middle sound. Trace the whole word.

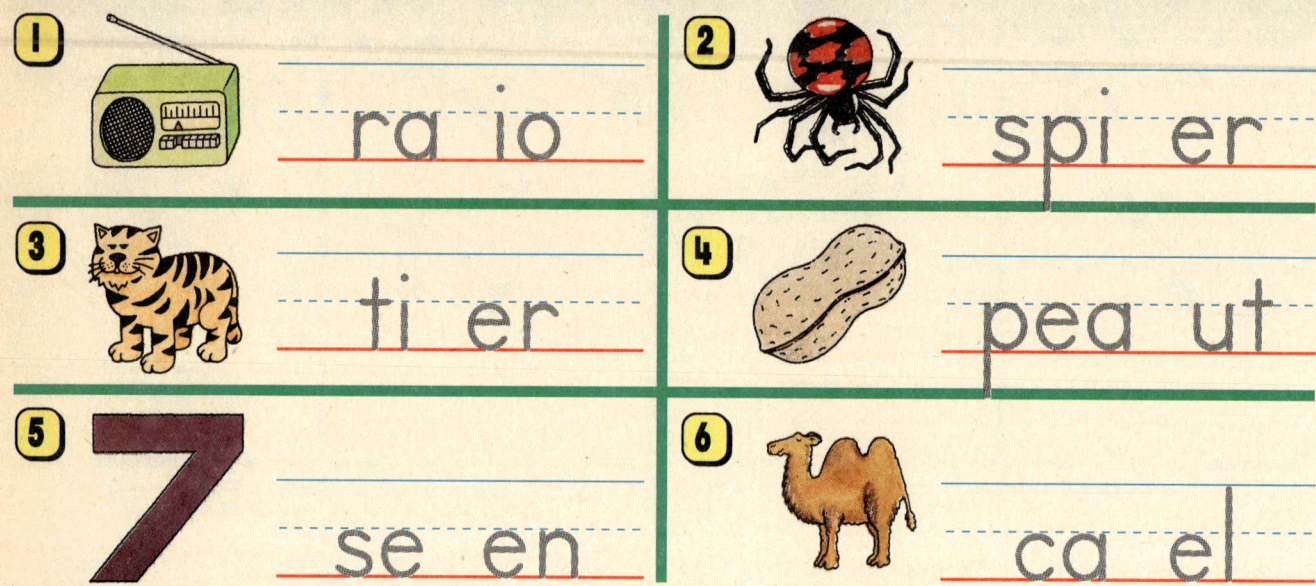

1 

ra _ io

2 

spi _ er

3 

ti _ er

4 

pea _ ut

5 7

se _ en

6 

ca _ el

Now try this!

Say the name of each picture. Print its missing letter on the line. Trace the whole word. Do what the sentences tell you to do.

7 

dra _ on

Color it red.

8 

ca _ in

Color it brown.

9 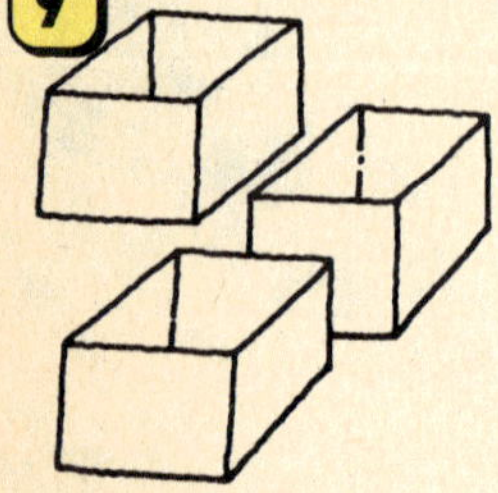

bo _ es

Color them blue.

10 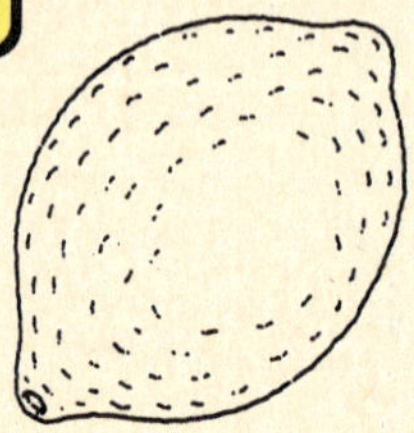

le _ on

Color it yellow.

Try this!

Say the name of each picture. Print its missing letter on the line. Trace the whole word. Then do what the sentences tell you to do.

1

Color it red. wa on

2

Color it yellow. un

3
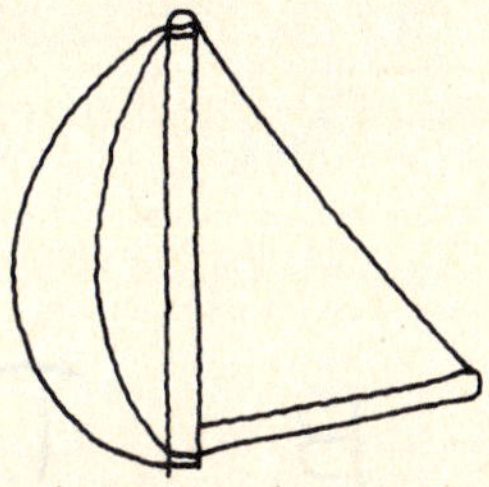
Color it green. sai

4

Color it blue. ra io

5

Color it yellow. us

6

Color it green. lea

7

Color it red. ro ot

8
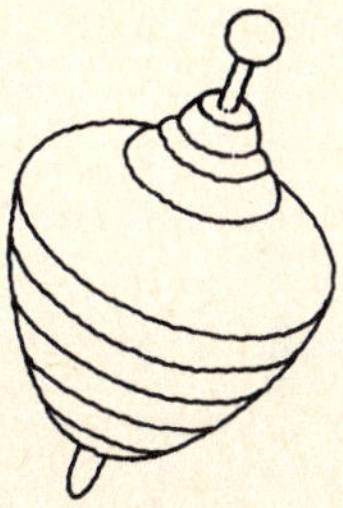
Color it blue. op

Here's what to do!

Say the name of each picture. Print the letters for its beginning, middle, and ending sounds.

1 

b l n

2 

w G n

3 

c i T

4 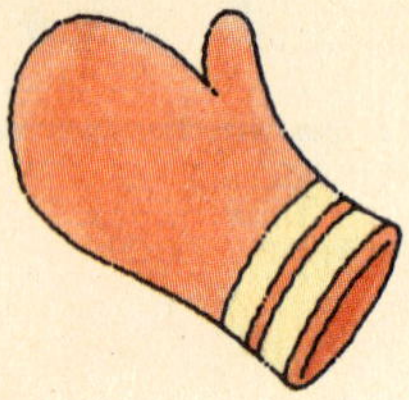

M n T

5 

c a M

6 

r b T

7 

L M n

8 

T Y r

9 

S v n

10 

c b n

11 

r b n

12 

w i n

What kind of jam can't you eat?

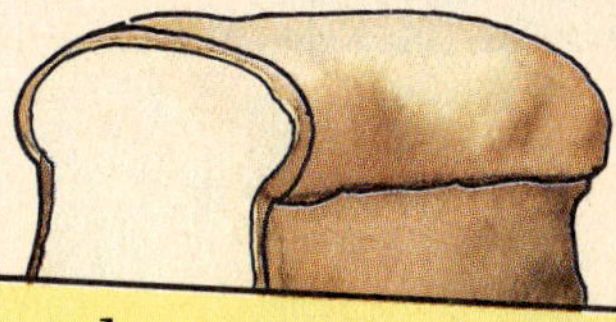

Here's what to do!

Circle the name of each picture.

If a word or syllable has only one vowel, and it comes at the beginning or between two consonants, the vowel is usually short. You can hear the short **a** sound in **jam.**

1. hat ham
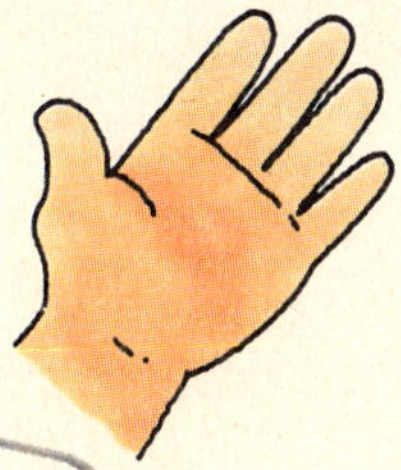
hand had

2. bag hat
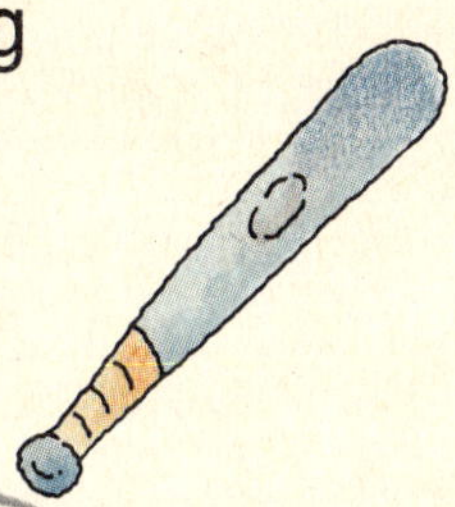
bat bad

3. camp lad

lap lamp

4. sad back
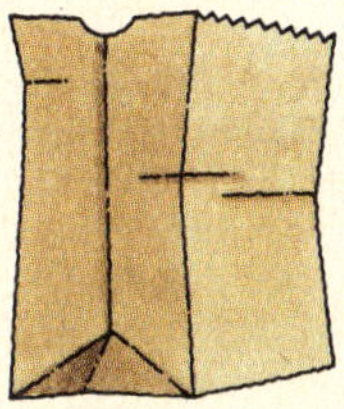
bag bat

5. cat cap

cab can

6. and an

at ant

7. mat man
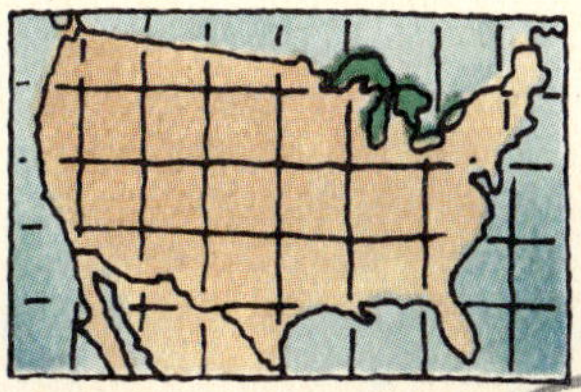
pan map

8. cat can

cab cap

9. mad ram

rack mat

Answer: A traffic jam.

Here's what to do!

Circle the rhyming words in each box. Draw a picture of the word that does not rhyme.

1 cat fan hat mat	2 Max tax bag wax	3 cap tap map cab
4 sack hand back tack	5 bag rag cap tag	6 sand land pan band
7 ham fan ran can	8 sad bat bad had	9 quack cat sack back
10 hand land lamp sand	11 pan fan Dan hat	12 sat ax pat fat

Here's what to do!

Print the name of each picture. Print a word that rhymes with it. Then do what the sentences tell you to do.

1

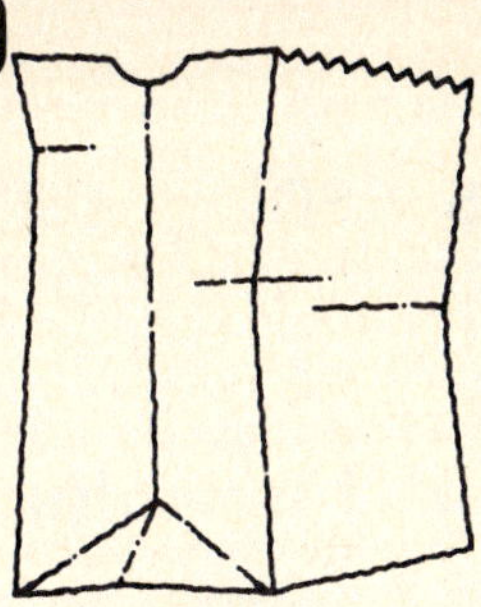

Color the bag red.

2

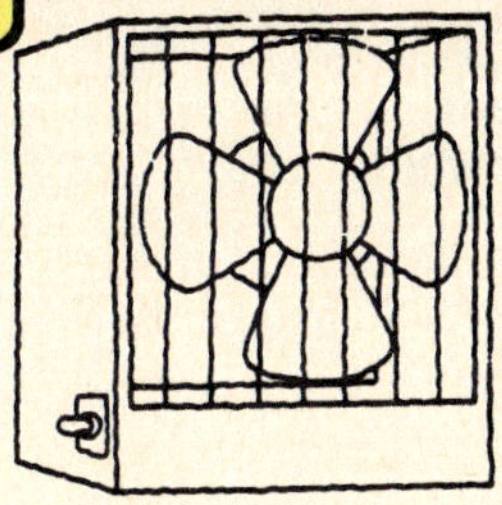

Color the fan green.

3

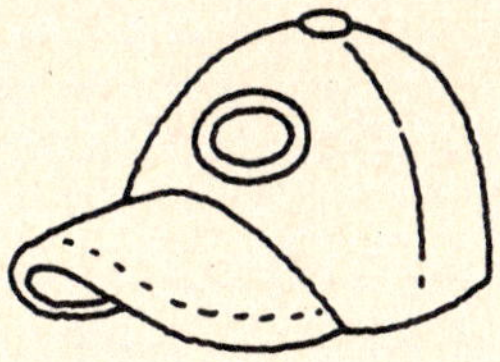

Color the cap red.

4

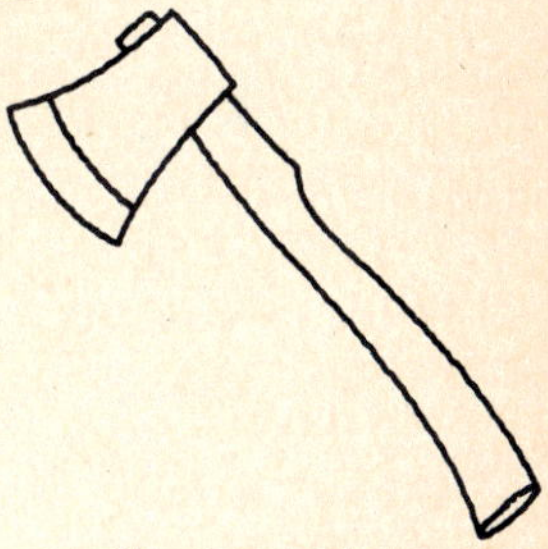

Color the ax blue.

5

Color the cat black.

6

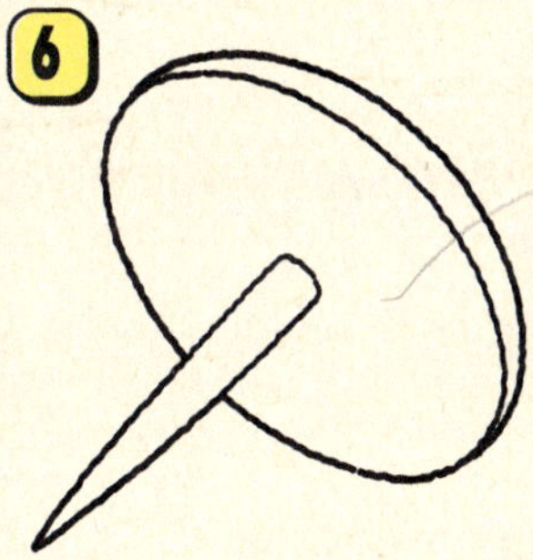

Color the tack yellow.

7

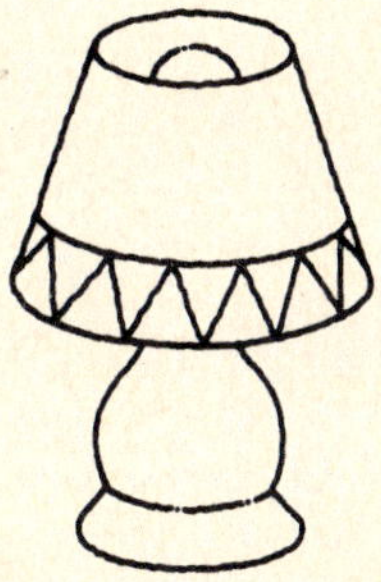

Color the lamp green and blue.

8

Color the ram black and yellow.

Here's what to do!

Circle the word that will finish each sentence. Print it on the line.

1. I am Sam and my cat is ______________ . camp Pat cart
2. Pat likes milk and ______________ food. class sat cat
3. She eats a lot but she is not ______________ . van fat lamp
4. She likes to lick my ______________ . hand gas band
5. Pat likes to sit on my ______________ . lap ham Sam
6. Pat does not like to have a ______________ . gap bath rack
7. She runs away as ______________ as she can. fast class bass
8. I ______________ always find her. can past fast
9. She takes a nap on a ______________ . mast mat fat
10. She takes a ______________ on Dad's lap. ran sat nap
11. I ______________ happy that Pat is my cat. can am as

Little kitty visits the big city.

Here's what to do!

Circle the name of each picture.

If a word or syllable has only one vowel, and it comes at the beginning or between two consonants, the vowel is usually short. You can hear the short **i** sound in **kitty** and **big.**

1

sack
milk
mill
tap

2

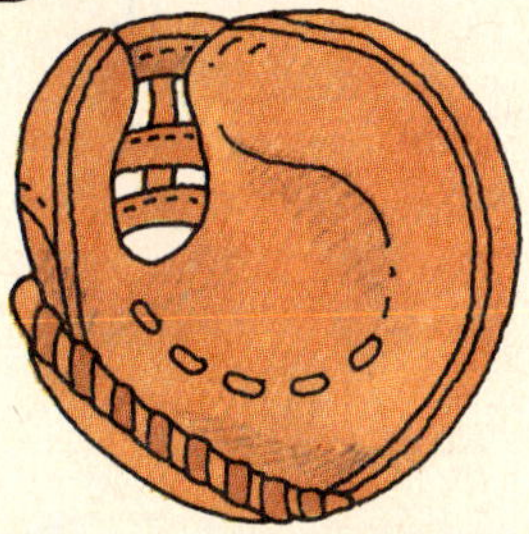

mitt
fat
mat
mill

3

wind
tag
wig
wag

4

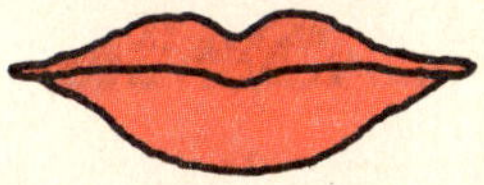

lap
lips
nap
dill

5

bag
pig
fig
pat

6

hill
bill
sill
hat

7

tax
six
fix
sat

8

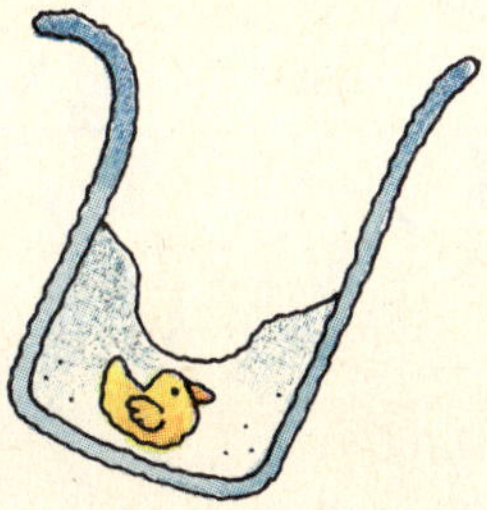

bill
bit
hat
bib

9

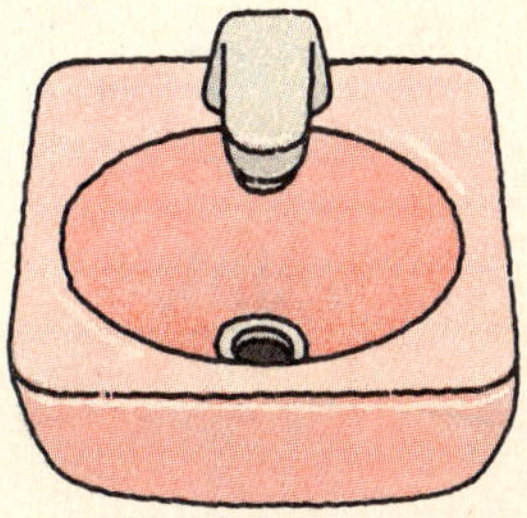

wink
sank
sink
pink

Try this!

Color the parts of each ball with rhyming words the same color.

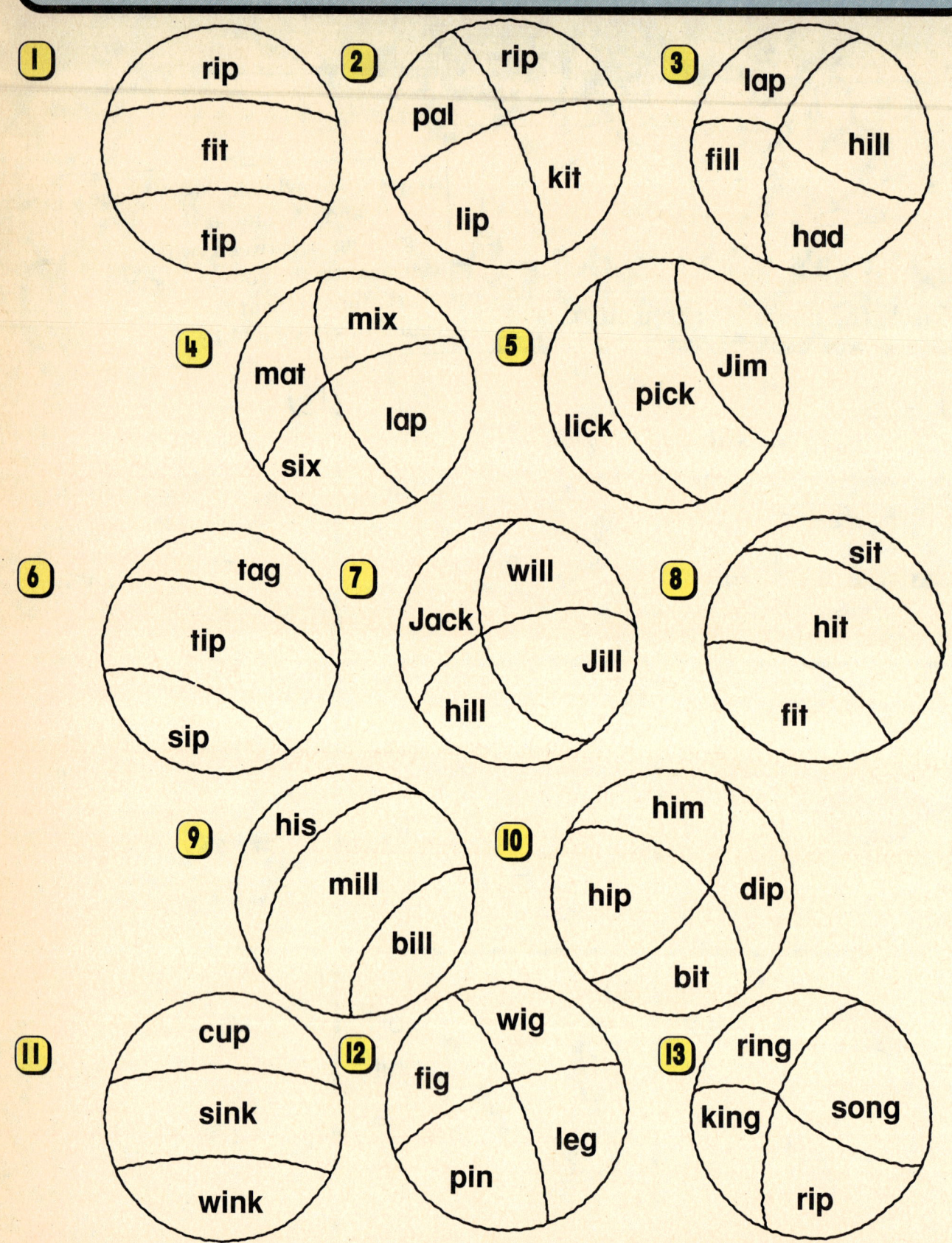

1. rip, fit, tip
2. rip, pal, kit, lip
3. lap, hill, fill, had
4. mix, mat, lap, six
5. Jim, pick, lick
6. tag, tip, sip
7. will, Jack, Jill, hill
8. sit, hit, fit
9. his, mill, bill
10. him, hip, dip, bit
11. cup, sink, wink
12. wig, fig, leg, pin
13. ring, king, song, rip

Do it this way!

Print the name of each picture. Then print a word that rhymes with it.

1

2

3

4

5
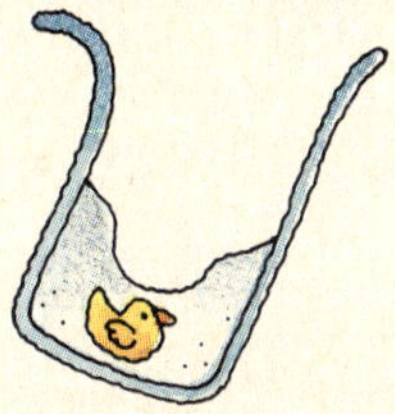

6

7
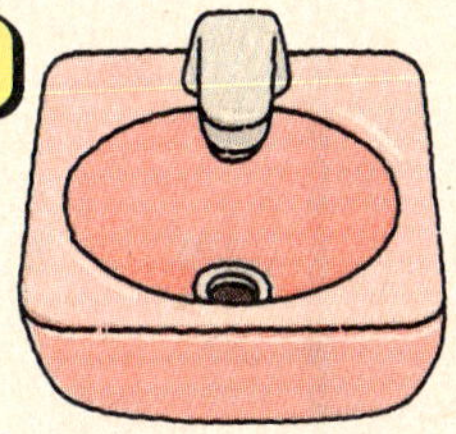

8

9
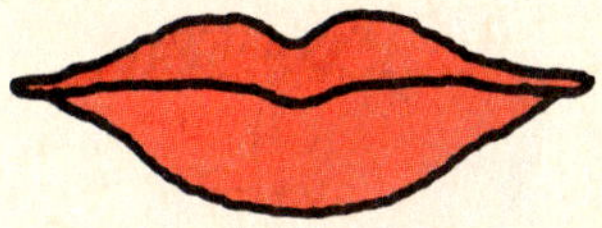

10

11

12

Here's what to do!

Circle the word that answers each riddle. Print it on the line.

1 It can swim.
What is it?

fast fish
fix fat

2 We drink it.
What is it?

mitt man
milk mat

3 It comes after five.
What is it?

sink sad
sat six

4 It rhymes with **bill.**
What is it?

hit hat
hill ham

5 Lunch goes on it.
What is it?

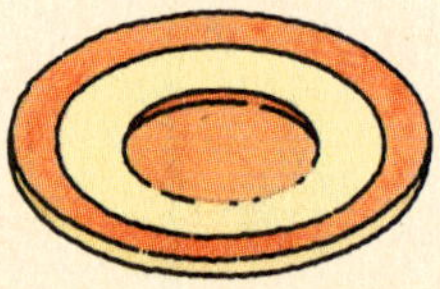

dad dish
dig did

6 It has a funny tail.
What is it?

pin pig
pal pat

7 It fits on a finger.
What is it?

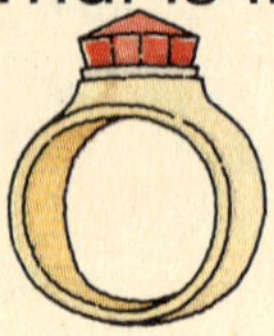

rank rat
rip ring

8 A baby wears this.
What is it?

bib bad
bill bat

9 We play ball with it.
What is it?

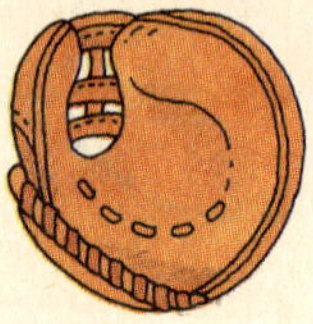

mat mitt
map mix

Here's what to do!

Read the words that begin each sentence. Use all of the words on the right to finish the sentence. Print them on the lines.

1	It is time to ______________________ .	a trip plan
2	We will camp ______________________ .	Bill Uncle with
3	Pam can ______________________ .	a find map
4	Zack and Pam will ______________________ .	snacks the fix
5	What will we pack ______________________ ?	in bags our
6	Will our bags fit ______________________ ?	in van the
7	Our dog Wags ______________________ .	will tag along
8	The trip we take ______________________ .	fun be will

Here's what to do!

Circle the word that will finish each sentence. Print it on the line.

1	I am fishing ________ Uncle Jim.	ham	with	gift
2	We ________ to catch a basket of fish.	hand	fin	plan
3	I put a ________ worm on my hook.	hit	fat	tack
4	Soon a fish will ________ by.	dish	swim	mat
5	I feel a tug on my line at ________.	fast	last	bat
6	A fish just ________ my bait.	hat	fix	bit
7	It is so big I can hardly ________ it.	lid	limb	lift
8	Uncle Jim helps me pull it ________.	pan	in	fill
9	This ________ will make a nice big meal.	fish	wash	fins
10	We will cook it in a ________.	pan	list	past
11	We ________ make fish and chips.	can	cast	cups
12	We will put the fish on a ________.	inch	dish	ant

Snug as a bug in a rug.

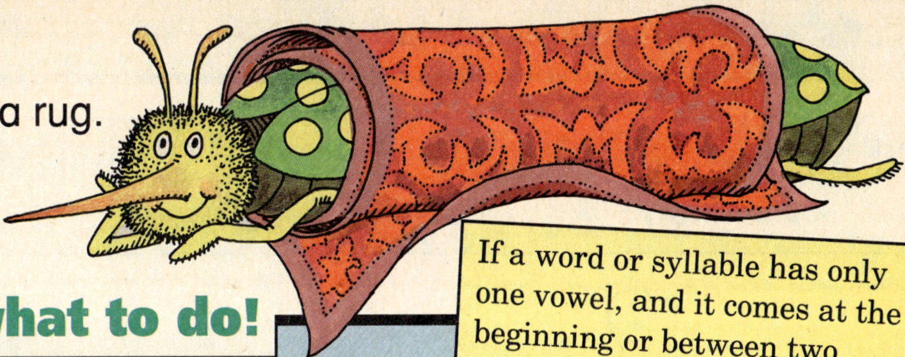

Here's what to do!

Circle the name of each picture. Print the vowel you hear in the word you circled.

If a word or syllable has only one vowel, and it comes at the beginning or between two consonants, the vowel is usually short. You can hear the short **u** sound in **bug** and **rug.**

1. cap cup kit

2. gas gull gum

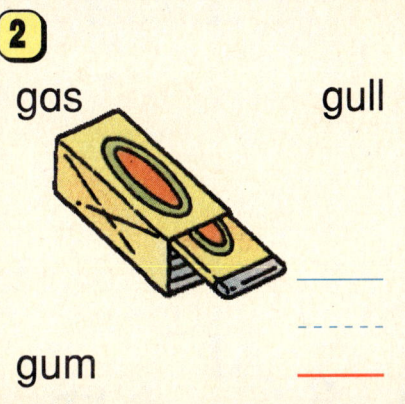

3. Dick duck dad

4. can cup cap
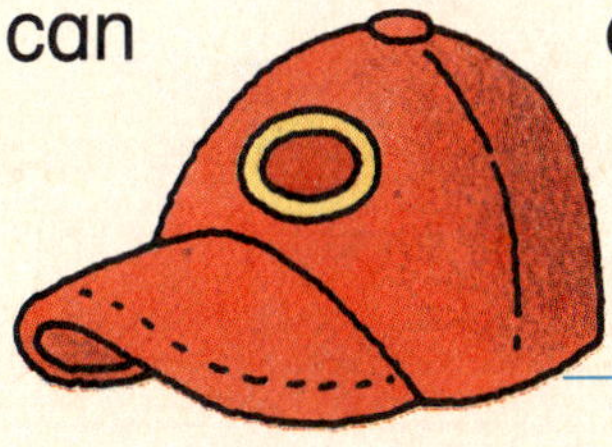

5. as bun bus

6. tug tip bug

7. but nut nap

8. sun sum dim

9. tab bin bat
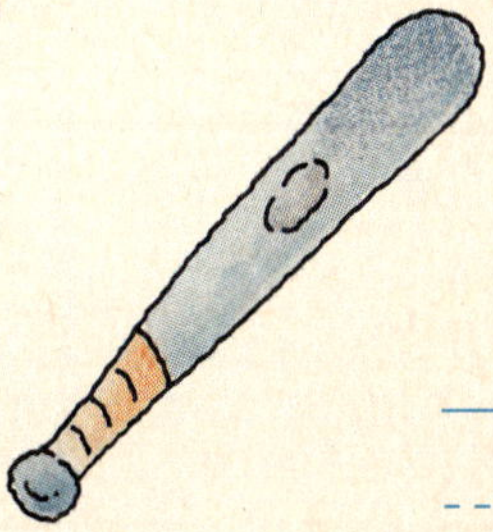

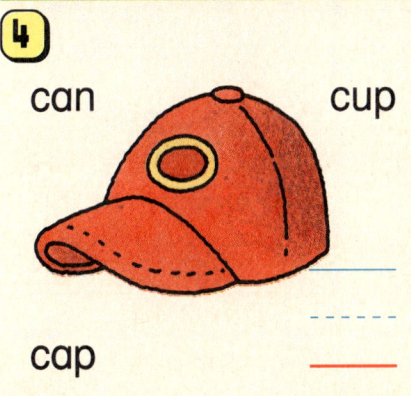

Here's what to do!

Find the word in the box that names each picture. Print it on the line.

bun	cup	rug	bus	bug	sun
gum	hug	hut	tub	jug	duck

1

2

3

4
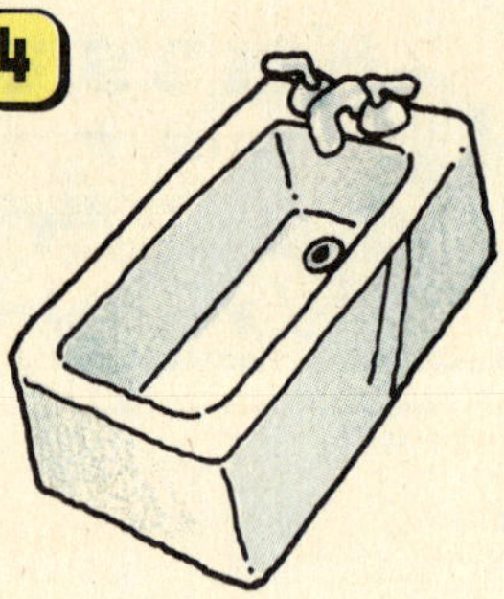

5

6

7

8
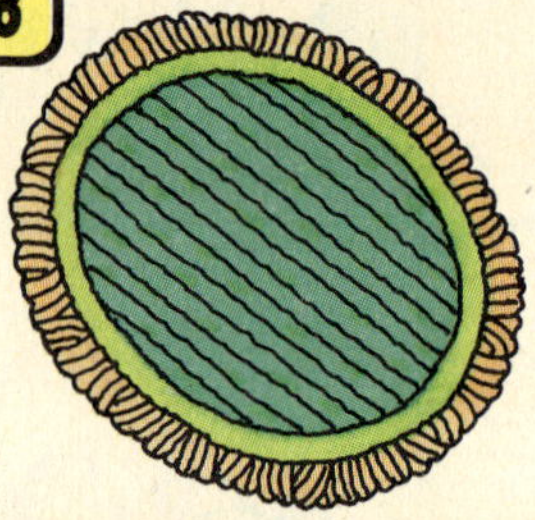

9

10

11

12

Here's what to do!

Circle the word that answers each riddle. Print it on the line.

1. My name rhymes with **hug.** What am I?

bus tub
bag bug

2. I am good to eat. What am I?

big bun
fun run

3. This is fun to do. What is it?

just lump
map jump

4. You take a bath in me. What am I?

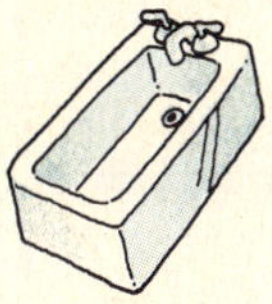

ran tub
bun rug

5. You can ride in me. What am I?

bud big
bus us

6. I shine on you. What am I?

sun but
sit fun

7. I say, "Quack, quack." What am I?

tack luck
pup duck

8. You can eat me. What am I?

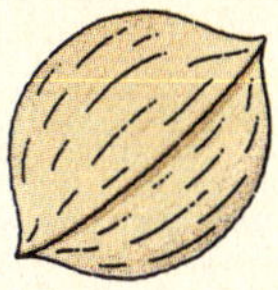

cut fit
fun nut

9. We like to chew it. What is it?

just bat
gum must

Here's what to do!

Circle the word that will finish each sentence. Print it on the line.

1	Today there was a fuss on the ________.	run bus must
2	A ________ jumped on Gus.	us bug hug
3	Gus jumped ________.	run cup up
4	Then it jumped on ________.	bus hug Russ
5	I saw the bug ________ on the window.	just jump rust
6	It was ________ a little bug.	just cup up
7	It liked to ________ up and down the window.	rug run cup
8	The bug ________ like to ride on the bus.	run us must

Try this!

Make new words by changing the vowels. Print them on the lines.

	a	i	u
1	fan	fin	
2	bad		
3	ham		
4	hat		
5	as		
6	bag		
7	rag		
8	bat		

Here's what to do!

Fill in the bubble beside the answer to each question.

1 Can a cup run?	○ Yes	○ No
2 Is the sun black?	○ Yes	○ No
3 Can a cat run fast?	○ Yes	○ No
4 Can a big pig sing for you?	○ Yes	○ No
5 Can we nap in a tan van?	○ Yes	○ No
6 Can a man run up a hill?	○ Yes	○ No
7 Is a green rug red?	○ Yes	○ No
8 Can you sit on a bus?	○ Yes	○ No
9 Can a little pup run fast and jump?	○ Yes	○ No
10 Can you fill a pan with milk?	○ Yes	○ No
11 Can a doll jump on the bus?	○ Yes	○ No
12 Can a pig go as fast as a cab?	○ Yes	○ No
13 Can you rub your hands?	○ Yes	○ No
14 Is a happy cat sad?	○ Yes	○ No
15 Can a bus be big?	○ Yes	○ No
16 Can a bug sit in the mud?	○ Yes	○ No
17 Can a bug lift a bus?	○ Yes	○ No
18 Is a little doll as big as a bus?	○ Yes	○ No

Such A Rush!

This book belongs to

_______________.

1

Nam runs down the hill as fast as he can.
The wind tugs at his cap.
"If I were a bug, this wind would lift me up," thinks Nam.

3

Nam stands up. Mud is on his pants and his hands.
If I were a pig, I would like all this mud," thinks Nam.

6

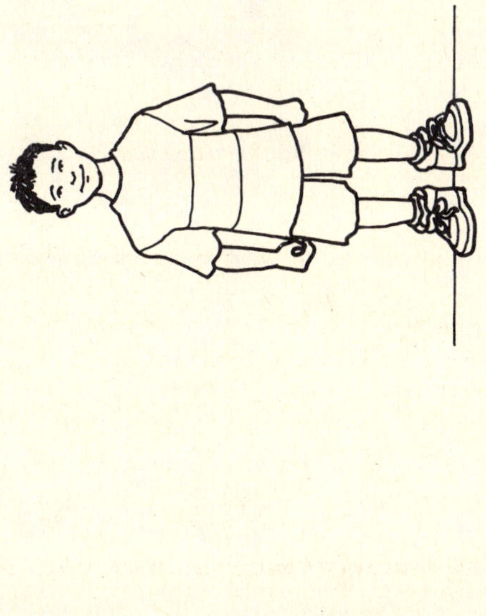

What will Nam wear the next time it rains?
Dress Nam for a rainy day.

8

FOLD

FOLD

"Hurry up, Nam!" says Dad. "Don't miss the bus."
Nam is in such a rush, he forgets his raincoat and umbrella.

2

Fat rain drops hit Nam and drip down his back.
"If I were a duck, I would like getting wet," thinks Nam.

4

Nam is wet to the skin! "I'm not a bug or a duck.
I'm not a fish or a pig," he says. "I'm a wet, muddy kid.
Next time, I won't forget my raincoat and umbrella!"

7

Then, Nam slips on the slick path.
Splat! He falls down in a mud puddle.
"If I were a fish, I could swim in this puddle," thinks Nam.

5

FOLD

Pop goes the popcorn.
Pop, pop, pop!
Pop goes the popcorn.
Hot, hot, hot!

Here's what to do!

Find the word in the box that names each picture. Print it on the line.

If a word or syllable has only one vowel, and it comes at the beginning or between two consonants, the vowel is usually short. You can hear the short **o** sound in **pop** and **hot.**

top	mop	pot	box	Tom	sock
hot	doll	fox	lock	rock	pop

1 

2 

3 

4 

5 

6 

7 

8 

9 

10 

11 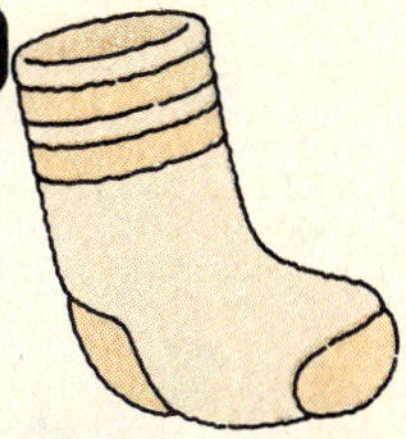

12 

Do it this way!

Circle the name of each picture.

1

fox
cob
fox
six

2

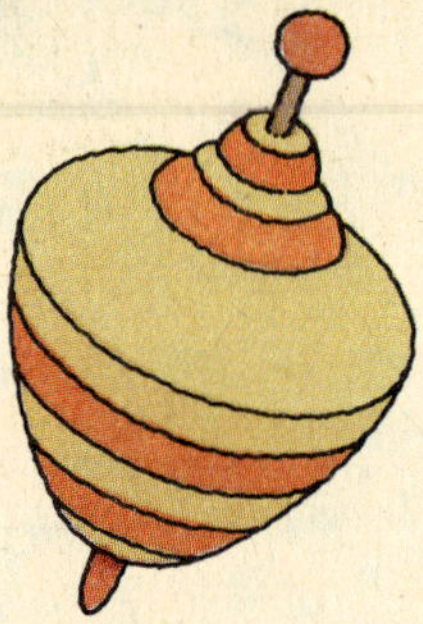

pot
top
tap
pit

3

bill
sill
dill
doll

4

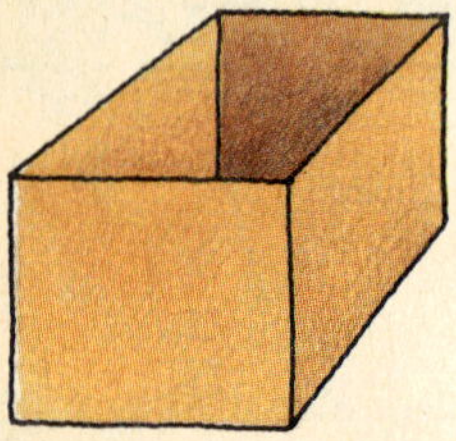

fox
fix
box
bat

5

dog
dug
dig
pot

6

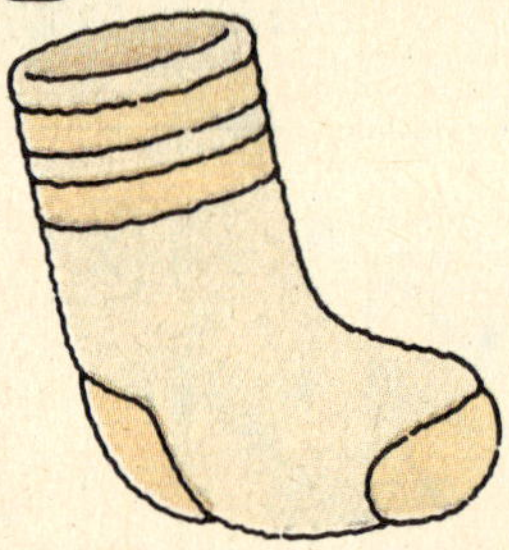

rock
sit
sack
sock

7

pig
pop
pup
pat

8

lag
log
bug
lot

9

luck
lock
lick
lack

10

mop
map
mud
milk

11

hat
hit
hot
hut

12

fix
tax
ax
ox

Try this!

Fill in the bubble beside the sentence that tells about the picture. Then draw a box around each short **o** word in the sentences.

1

- ◯ The fox is not on the log.
- ◯ The fox is in the log.
- ◯ The fox is on the log.
- ◯ The fox is under the log.

2

- ◯ Rob lost his socks.
- ◯ Rob sat on a big rock.
- ◯ Rob is on the big log.
- ◯ Rob has a big rock in his hand.

3

- ◯ The dog ran to the box.
- ◯ The mop is not in the box.
- ◯ I will hop on the log.
- ◯ See the doll in the box.

4

- ◯ I got the mop for Don.
- ◯ Jill has the big top.
- ◯ The big top is on the mop.
- ◯ The top is in Bob's hand.

5

- ◯ The hot pot is on the table.
- ◯ Dot is not holding a hot pot.
- ◯ Dot is holding a hot pot.
- ◯ The milk in the pot is not hot.

Here's what to do!

Circle the name of each picture.

1
six fix

sit sun

2
bun hit
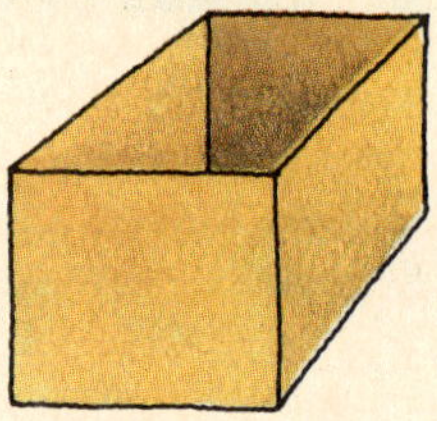
box fox

3
tan fan

fun fin

4
cup cap

kit can

5
sick sock
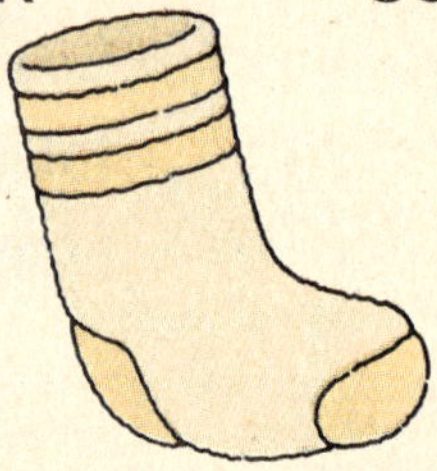
son sack

6
rock luck
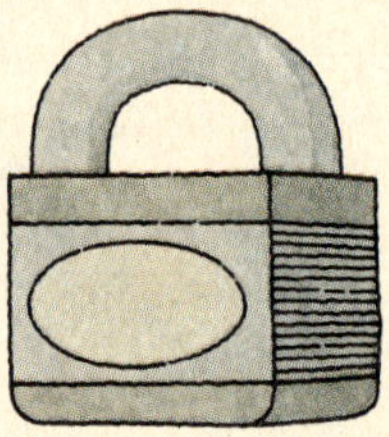
lock sock

7
fix fox

box fun

8
pin top
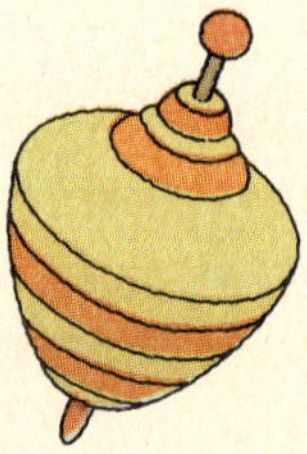
pot tip

9
pot dug

dog log

10
hot cot

pot hut

11
rock sock

duck lock

12
pig pop

pat pot

Here's what to do!

Print the name of each picture on the line.

1

2

3

4

5

6
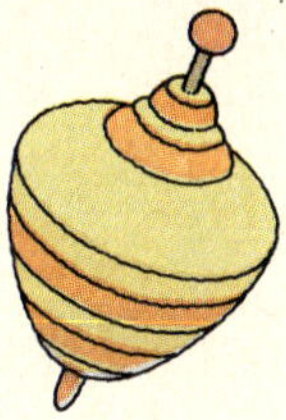

7

8

9
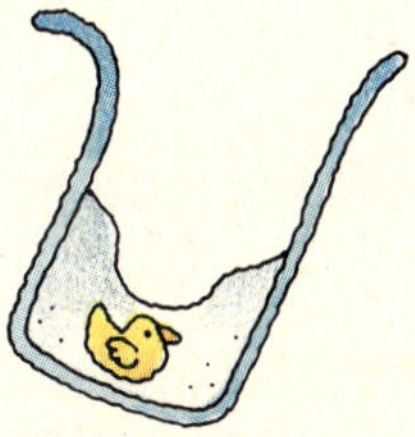

10

11

12

13
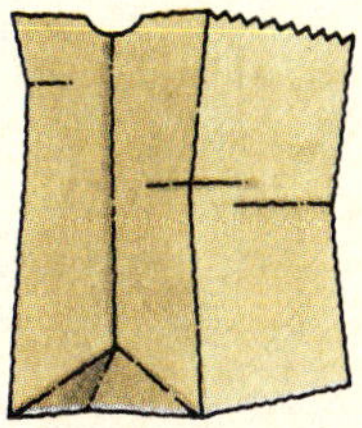

14

15

16

Do it this way!

Find the word in the box that will finish each sentence. Print it on the line.

1. Pam will make ____________ for us.
2. Dot hopes she ____________ make soup.
3. Bob wants ____________ dogs.
4. Uncle ____________ wants ham.
5. All the ____________ want stew.
6. Let's ____________ Pam what she made.

Dan
kids
will
ask
hot
lunch

7. ____________ made a pot full of soup.
8. There is a wet ____________ on the floor.
9. Dot ____________ and can't stop.
10. She ____________ the pot.
11. The soup spills ____________ the floor.
12. Now Dot has to mop it ____________ .

spot
slips
Pam
on
up
drops

What do you get when you wash your pet?

If a word or syllable has only one vowel, and it comes at the beginning or between two consonants, the vowel is usually short. You can hear the short **e** sound in **get** and **pet.**

Try this!

Say the name of each picture. Print the name on the line.

1 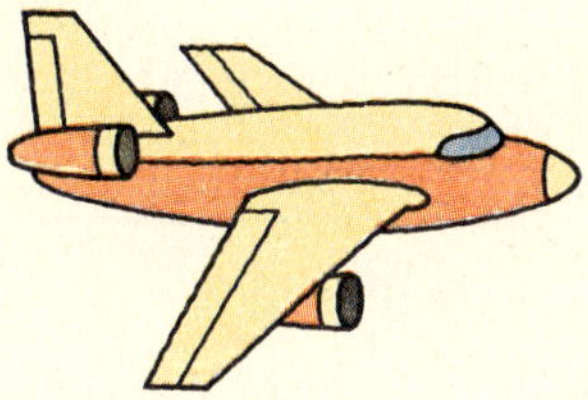

2 

3 

4 

5 

6 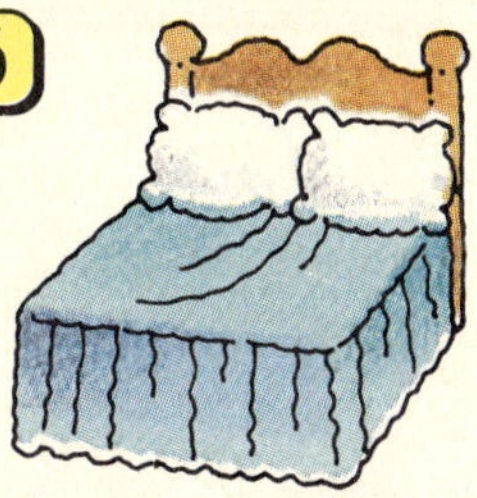

7 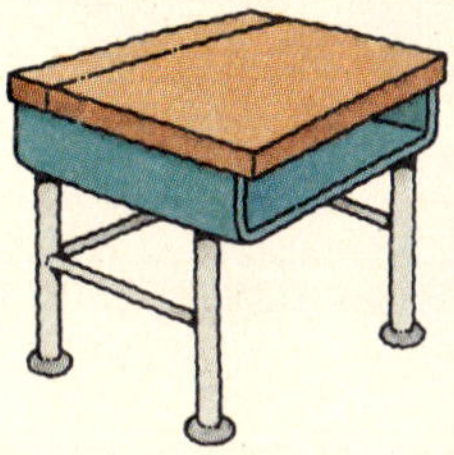

8 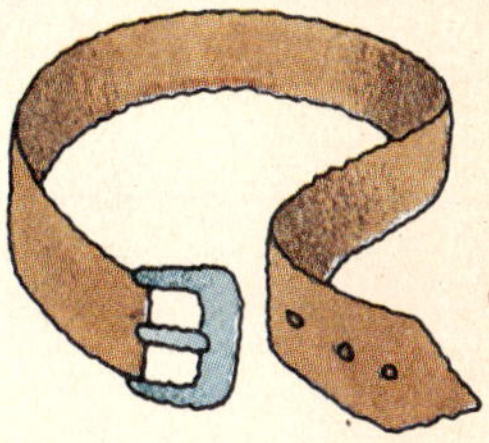

9 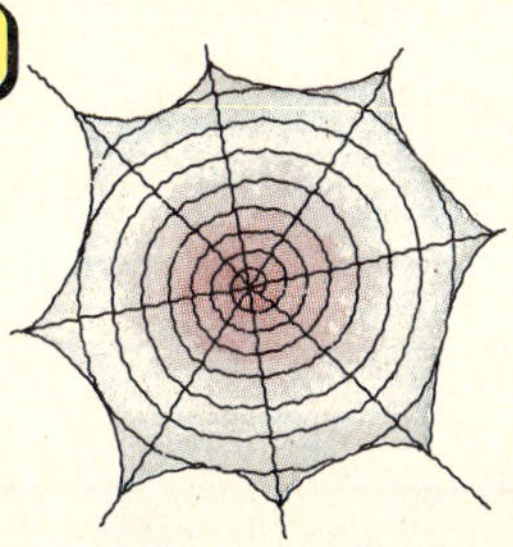

10 

11 

12 

Answer: Wet!

Here's what to do!

Print the name of each picture. Then do what the sentences tell you to do.

1

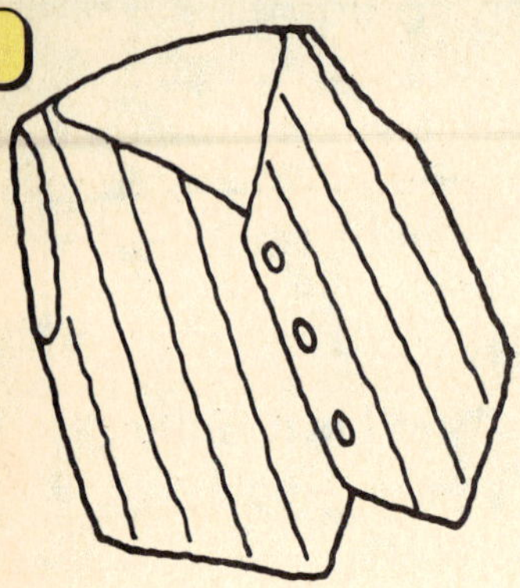

2

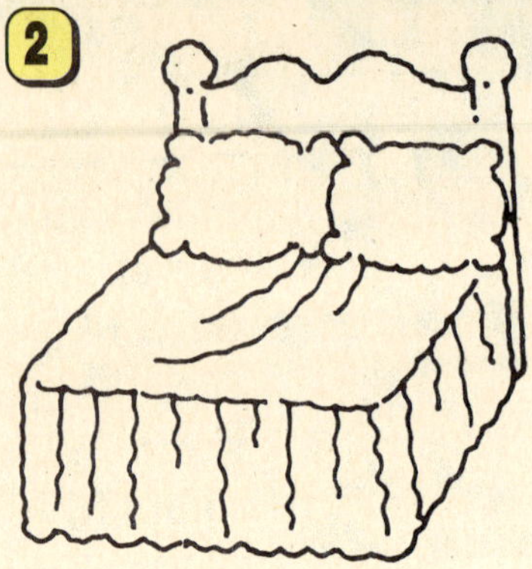

3

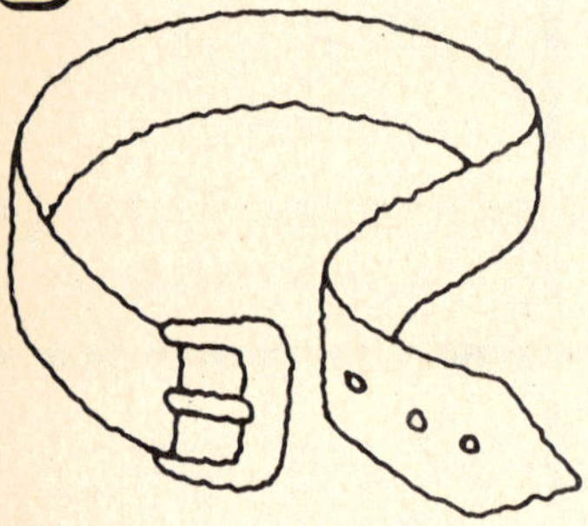

4

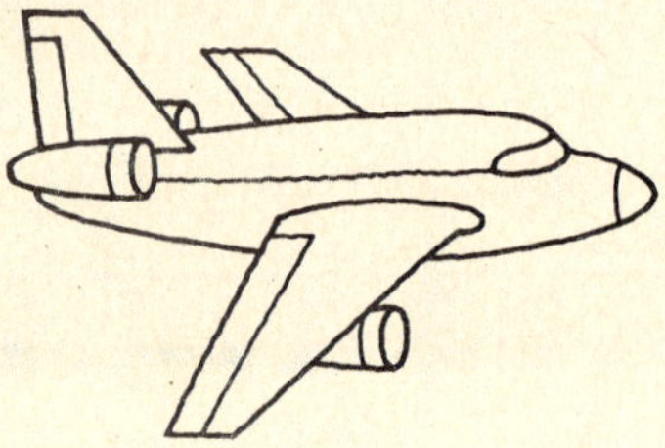

5

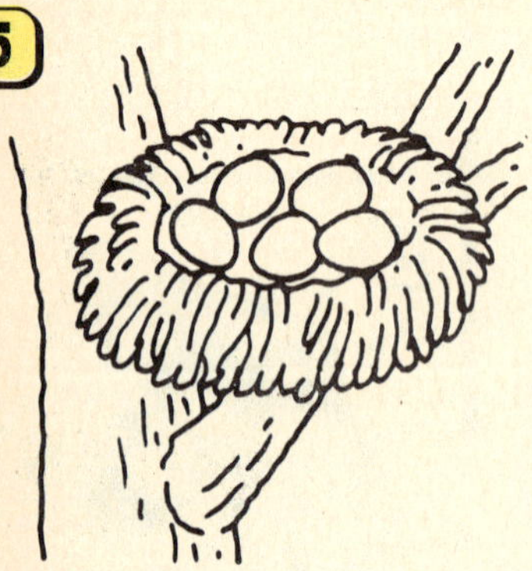

6

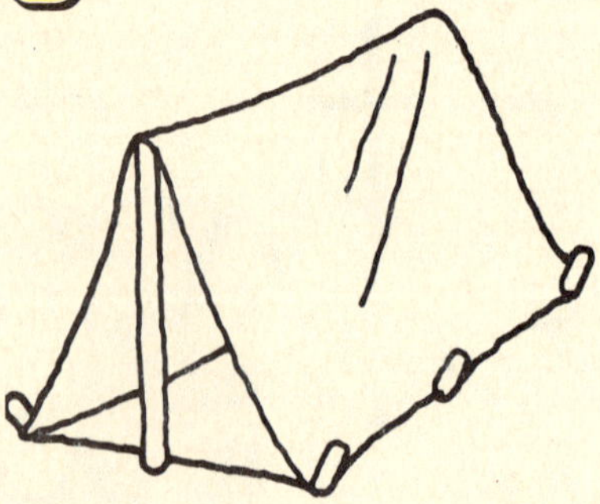

Find the bed.
Color it red and blue.

Find the jet.
Color it black.

Find the nest.
Color three eggs red and two eggs blue.

Find the tent.
Color it yellow.

Find the belt.
Color it green.

Find the vest.
Color it red and black.

Do it this way!

Fill in the bubble below the word that will finish each sentence. Print it on the line.

1. My name is ______. — men ○ Jeff ○ jet ○
2. I want to get a ______. — bet ○ pet ○ yet ○
3. I would like a pet dog ______. — rest ○ west ○ best ○
4. I will ______ take care of my pet. — help ○ bell ○ nest ○
5. I can take it to the ______. — vet ○ bet ○ set ○
6. I will make sure it is ______. — get ○ fed ○ bed ○
7. It will need a good ______. — bed ○ nest ○ best ○
8. I will ______ it in and out. — jet ○ test ○ let ○
9. I can dry it when it's ______. — net ○ wet ○ set ○
10. I will ______ it if I get it. — sled ○ pet ○ west ○
11. I might name my pet ______. — Pepper ○ fed ○ set ○
12. I will ______ Ned about my pet. — sell ○ tell ○ fell ○

Here's what to do!

Print the name of each picture on the line.

1 

2 

3 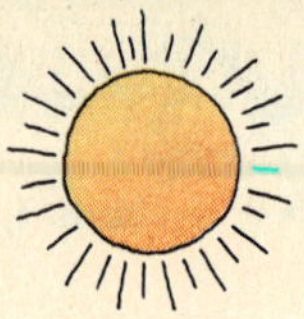

4 

5 

Now try this!

Answer each sentence by printing **yes** or **no** on the line.

6 You can rest in a bed.

7 You have ten fingers and ten toes.

8 A cat has six legs.

9 A big bus can jump up and down.

10 You can go fast in a jet.

11 An ant is as big as an ox.

12 Six is less than ten.

13 You can sit in a tent.

14 A hen can lay eggs.

Here's what to do!

Find the word that will finish each sentence. Print it on the line.

1. A crab can dig in the ______________.
2. A hen sits on a ______________.
3. A ______________ can live in a pen.
4. A spider spins a ______________.
5. A bug can be snug in a ______________.
6. A fish can ______________ in the water.

nest
swim
rug
web
sand
pig

7. My ______________ and I like to camp.
8. I help him ______________ up the tent.
9. I sleep on my ______________.
10. My dad sleeps ______________ a mat.
11. We have ______________ when we camp.

on
cot
set
fun
dad

Try this!

Look at each word. Change the vowel to make a new word. Print it on the line.

1 tug ______	2 tab ______	3 fox ______
4 rust ______	5 sand ______	6 tint ______

Now try this!

Find the word that will finish each sentence. Print it on the line.

hop
with
sun
fell
ran
mud
bed

7 After the rain, the ______ was shining.

8 I ______ out to play and have fun.

9 I slid in the wet ______ .

10 I ______ and landed with a thud.

11 Now I am covered ______ mud.

12 It is time to ______ in the tub.

13 Then it will be time to go to ______ .

The Best Pet for You

This book belongs to

Remember that a pet needs to be fed.
A big pet like a dog or a cat must be fed every day.
It needs fresh water to drink, too.

Pets can't sit still.
A dog needs to run and jump and romp.
A bird needs to fly.
A cat likes to play.

Write one or two sentences about your pet or a pet you would like to have.

Kids have all kinds of pets.
What is the best pet for you?
Here are some things to think about
before you get a pet.

2

If a pet gets sick, it may need to go to a vet.
Taking care of a pet is a big job.
It will need love and care all its life.

7

FOLD

A pet needs a snug home, too.
Fish need a tank. A rabbit needs a
hutch. A bird needs a cage.
A puppy or a kitten likes a soft bed.

4

A pet's home must be kept clean.
A fish tank must be scrubbed.
A hamster cage needs to be cleaned.
A litter box needs to be kept fresh.

5

FOLD

Jane wants the rain to stop today.
She wants to go outside and play.

Here's what to do!

Find the word that will finish each sentence. Print it on the line.

If a word or syllable has two vowels, the first vowel usually stands for the long sound, and the second vowel is silent. If the first vowel is **a,** the word has the long **a** sound. You can hear the long **a** sound in **Jane, rain,** and **play.**

away
face
games
came
play

1. Jane made a ______________ when she saw it rain.
2. She wanted the rain to go ______________.
3. She had planned to ______________ outside.
4. Then Jake ______________ over.
5. Jake and Jane played ______________ inside.

rain
ate
wait
cake

6. The children had to ______________ for the rain to stop.
7. Jane's sister baked a ______________.
8. Jane and Jake ______________ a piece.
9. At last the ______________ stopped and they ran outside.

Here's what to do!

Circle the word that will finish each sentence. Print it on the line.

1. It is a nice ____________ today. day rain rake
2. May we go to the ____________? bake take lake
3. Let's ____________ a picnic lunch. mail take say
4. We can bring a ____________ and shovel. pail mail rain
5. We could ____________ sand castles. make wake fake
6. Our dog ____________ could come, too. take Kate save
7. Is there any ____________ we can go today? say tail way

Now try this!

Circle each long **A** word in the box. Then print the name of each picture on the line.

tap	tape	cap	cape	at	ate
mail	mat	rain	gate	hay	ham

8. 
____

9. 
____

10. 
____

11. 
____

I like pie.
Apple pie,
peach pie,
cherry pie.
I like pie.

If a word or syllable has two vowels, the first vowel usually stands for the long sound, and the second vowel is silent. If the first vowel is **i,** the word has the long **i** sound. You can hear the long **i** sound in **like** and **pie.**

Here's what to do!

Circle the name of each picture.

1

dim dime

2

pig pile

3

bike big

4

bib bite

Now try this!

Circle the word that will finish each sentence. Then print it on the line.

5 Mike likes to ride a ________.
bit bike bite

6 Diane likes to ________.
hike hill hit

7 Ike likes cherry ________.
pie pig pine

8 Kyle likes to fly a ________.
bite hive kite

9 Fido likes to ________.
rid ride hive

10 We all like lunch ________.
tide time tip

Here's what to do!

Circle the word that will finish each sentence. Print it on the line.

1. A turtle can ______ inside its shell. dime time hide
2. A ______ can hide in a den very well. lion tile pie
3. My dog can hide behind our ______ . likes bikes dives
4. A bee can hide in its ______ . hive time kite
5. A spider can hide anywhere it ______ . pine mine likes
6. I ______ to hide things here and there. like mile dime
7. No one can ______ them anywhere. kind find pile

Now try this!

Circle each long **I** word in the box. Print the name of each picture on the line.

dim	dime	pin	pine	rid	ride
mine	tie	sit	kite	nine	line

8. 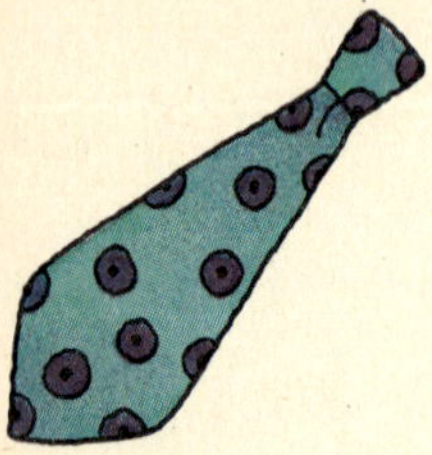
______

9. 
______

10. 
______

11. 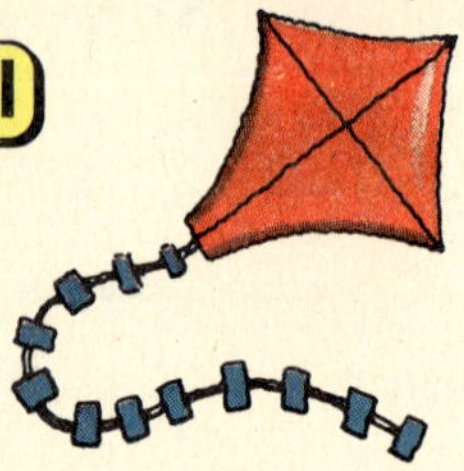
______

Do it this way!

Circle the word each sentence tells about. Print it on the line.

1	We fly this on a windy day.	______	rake	kite	kit
2	A dog can wag it.	______	tail	pail	pat
3	We did it to Pat's cake.	______	at	late	ate
4	Jane has a can of it.	______	pat	pain	paint
5	We like to ride boats on this.	______	bake	mile	lake
6	We like to eat it.	______	bit	pie	pat
7	We can ride it.	______	bill	bat	bike
8	We do this to shoes.	______	tip	tie	time
9	We can save this.	______	like	dime	dip
10	A wet day has this.	______	rain	rake	ran
11	We play this.	______	bat	gate	game
12	A clock tells this.	______	time	Tim	take

Try this!

Read the words in the balloons. Print the long **A** words under Kay's name. Print the long **I** words under Mike's name.

Sue and Luke are playing flutes.

Here's what to do!

Circle the answer **Yes** or **No** for each sentence. Then circle the long **U** word in each sentence. Print it on the line.

If a word or syllable has two vowels, the first vowel usually stands for the long sound, and the second vowel is silent. If the first vowel is **u,** the word has the long **u** sound. You can hear the long **u** sound in **Sue, Luke,** and **flutes.**

1. A red vase is blue. ____ Yes No
2. We can get toothpaste in a tube. ____ Yes No
3. A baby lion is a cube. ____ Yes No
4. A mule has nine tails. ____ Yes No
5. You stick things together with glue. ____ Yes No
6. We can eat a suit. ____ Yes No
7. A rule is a top that can sing. ____ Yes No
8. We play a song with a flute. ____ Yes No
9. We can hum a tune. ____ Yes No

Do it this way!

Read the words in the box. Print the short **U** words under Short **U**. Print the long **U** words under Long **U**.

cute	must	bug	duck
jump	suit	tune	bump
tube	dug	glue	mule
nut	rule	use	hum
flute	luck	jug	blue

Short U	Long U

Do it this way!

Read each word. If the word has a long vowel, fill in the bubble beside **long.** If the word has a short vowel, fill in the bubble beside **short.**

1 late ○ long ○ short	2 June ○ long ○ short	3 mule ○ long ○ short
4 man ○ long ○ short	5 tube ○ long ○ short	6 ride ○ long ○ short
7 rain ○ long ○ short	8 pick ○ long ○ short	9 six ○ long ○ short
10 use ○ long ○ short	11 cute ○ long ○ short	12 cap ○ long ○ short
13 bat ○ long ○ short	14 time ○ long ○ short	15 fun ○ long ○ short
16 bake ○ long ○ short	17 lick ○ long ○ short	18 us ○ long ○ short
19 map ○ long ○ short	20 wide ○ long ○ short	21 gate ○ long ○ short
22 wipe ○ long ○ short	23 pie ○ long ○ short	24 tune ○ long ○ short
25 lap ○ long ○ short	26 ate ○ long ○ short	27 nut ○ long ○ short
28 up ○ long ○ short	29 fine ○ long ○ short	30 make ○ long ○ short

Here's what to do!

Circle the word that will finish each sentence. Print it on the line.

1. We ______________ to play music. ride like hike
2. It is a nice ______________ to spend a day. pay side way
3. June likes to play her ______________ . flute suit time
4. Jay can play his ______________ . bake tuba tub
5. Mike ______________ tunes on his uke. side sit plays
6. Sue plays a ______________ . bugle suit like
7. ______________ like to play my drum. It I Ice
8. We all sing ______________ . tunes times tiles
9. We can play ______________ in a parade. music suit fan
10. We hope our uniforms come on ______________ . tip cub time
11. We can play at a football ______________ , too! gum game gate

FOLD

The Duke Who Could Not Stay Awake

This book belongs to

______________________. 1

Draw a picture and write a sentence to tell what exercise will keep Luke awake. 8

FOLD

"Duke Luke must stay awake," they said. "Let's use ice cubes!"

"STOP! I know what will help Luke stay awake," called a little girl. "He needs fresh air and exercise." 6

He slept while musicians with bagpipes, flutes, and lutes played a tune. 3

Once upon a time, there was a duke named Luke.
He could not stay awake.
He could not rule his land.

2

And she was right!
Duke Luke ruled happily ever after.

7

FOLD

Bakers made huge plates of things for Luke to eat.
But nothing kept him awake.

4

They used a huge fan to make a breeze.
But still he slept.

5

FOLD

I know a silly mole in an overcoat,
Who rows a very little boat.

Do it this way!

Circle each long **O** word in the box.

If a word or syllable has two vowels, the first vowel usually stands for the long sound, and the second vowel is silent. If the first vowel is **o,** the word has the long **o** sound. You can hear the long **o** sound in **know, mole,** and **boat.**

rod	road	rode	cot	coat	got	goat
hope	hop	robe	rob	row	cost	coast

Now try this!

Find the word in the box that will finish each sentence. Print it on the line.

coat
owner
Rover
show
bone
bowl
nose

1. Rover poked his __________ into his bowl.
2. He hoped to find a __________ .
3. There was no bone in his __________ .
4. Then along came his __________ , Joe.
5. Something was in the pocket of Joe's __________ .
6. Joe said, "I have something to __________ you."
7. Oh, boy! It was a bone for __________ !

Here's what to do!

Circle the name of each picture.

1 

cot coat

2 

toad tad

3 

got goat

4 

note not

5 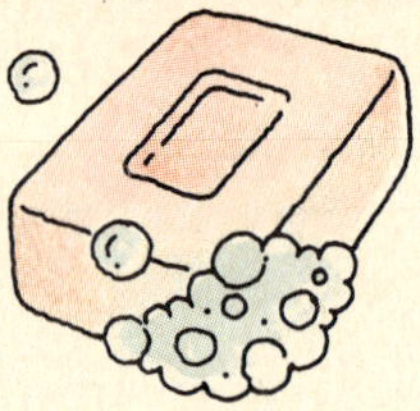

sap soap

6 

rope rot

Now try this!

Say the word in the box. Then read the sentence. To finish the sentence, think of a word that rhymes with the word in the box. Print the word on the line.

7 Joe was taking a ride in his ________. | coat

8 Joe's dog Rover wanted to ________, too. | no

9 Rover poked Joe with his ________. | rose

10 Joe told Rover to ________ into the boat. | top

11 Then Joe untied the ________. | hope

12 Finally, Joe began to ________. | bow

Here's what to do!

Print the name of each picture on the line.

1 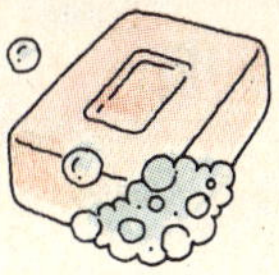

2 

3 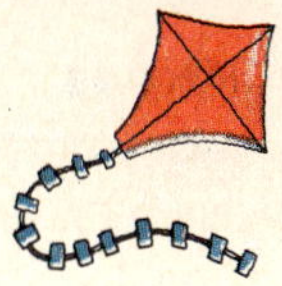

4 

5 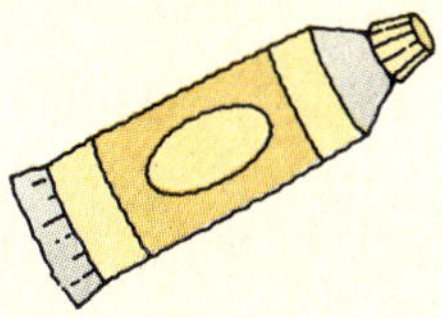

6 

Now try this!

Find the word in the box that will finish each sentence. Print it on the line.

make
cake
own
ice
tuna

7 Ruth likes to make ______ sandwiches.

8 Sue mixes fruit juice with ______ cubes.

9 Jake bakes carrot ______ .

10 It's fun to make our ______ lunch.

11 It would be more fun to ______ dinner.

Here's what to do!

Fill in the bubble beside the word that will finish each sentence. Print it on the line.

1. Tim had a nice ______________ outside. ○ Tim ○ time
2. He ______________ his bike. ○ rode ○ rod
3. He flew his ______________. ○ kite ○ kit
4. He played ______________ and seek with June. ○ hid ○ hide
5. Then ______________ and June came inside. ○ Tim ○ time
6. They ______________ some cookies. ○ mad ○ made
7. They ______________ every single bite. ○ ate ○ at
8. They decided to ______________ grape juice to make ice cubes. ○ use ○ us
9. Their grape ice ______________ tasted great! ○ cubs ○ cubes
10. Tim and June played ______________ the tail on the donkey. ○ pine ○ pin
11. Then they each made a paper ______________. ○ plan ○ plane
12. Tim told June, "I ______________ you had fun." ○ hope ○ hop

What do you need to play musical chairs?

If a word or syllable has two vowels, the first vowel usually stands for the long sound, and the second vowel is silent. If the first vowel is **e,** the word has the long **e** sound. You can hear the long **e** sound in **need** and **seat.**

Give this a try!

Circle the name of each picture.

1. 
set
seal
seed

2. 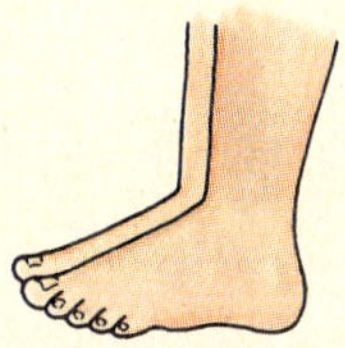
feel
fell
feet

3. 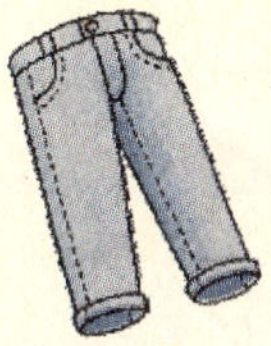
jays
jeans
jeeps

4. 
heel
hill
heat

5. 
beets
beds
beads

6. 
jet
jeep
Jean

Now try this!

Circle the word that will finish each sentence. Print it on the line.

7. Seals live in the ______________ . seat sea set

8. They ______________ fish. neat eat feet

9. We can teach ______________ tricks. east seals beets

10. Have you ______________ a seal show? set free seen

11. We will see one next ______________ . week met beak

Answer: Seats with a beat.

Do it this way!

Circle the long **E** word in each sentence. Then print it on the line.

1. I wore my new blue jeans.
2. I wanted them to stay clean.
3. It was hard for me to do.
4. My dog put his dirty feet on them.
5. Mud from the street splashed on them.
6. I sat on a seat that had gum on it.
7. My lunch box leaked on them.
8. At lunch, pea soup spilled on them.
9. Gus dropped his beans on them.
10. Then I ripped the knee.
11. After that, well, so much for my jeans.
12. I've never seen a bigger mess!

Can you think of other ways you can help save water?
Write a sentence telling how you can help.

8

Water

This book belongs to

1

Take shorter baths and showers.
Water plants and gardens in the morning or after the sun goes down.

6

We use water in our homes every day.
We need clean water for many things.

3

Water comes from the rain and the
2 snow that fills our lakes and streams.

Following these simple tips will help you use water wisely every day. 7

FOLD

If there isn't enough rain or snow, our water supply grows smaller.
That's why it's important not to waste
4 water.

Here are some tips for how you can help save water: Don't leave the water running when you brush your teeth. 5

FOLD

Try this!

Say the name of each picture. Print the vowel you hear on the first line. If the vowel is short, print an **S** on the second line. If the vowel is long, print an **L** on the second line.

1 

2 

3 

4 

5 

6 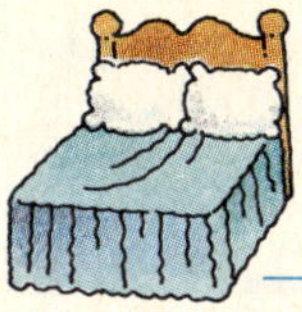

7 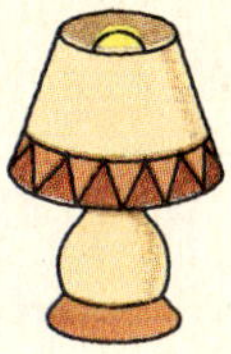

8 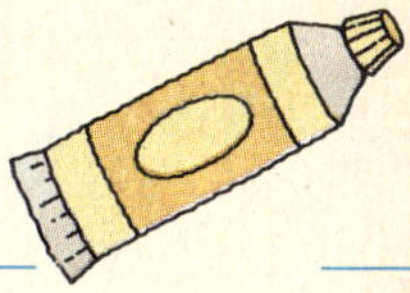

9 

10 

11 

12 

Now try this!

Finish the rhyming words.

13 hat mat sat

14 went d r

15 fun r b

16 gate l d

17 like b h

18 goat c b

Do it this way!

Change the first vowel in each word to make a new word. Print it on the line.

1. boat ________
2. sod ________
3. red ________
4. oar ________
5. hop ________
6. ran ________
7. cone ________
8. wide ________
9. bake ________
10. nip ________
11. tame ________
12. map ________

Now do this!

Find a word in the box that rhymes with each word. Print it on the line.

13. time ________
14. cube ________
15. rub ________
16. need ________
17. tape ________
18. bat ________
19. clue ________

tube
cub
blue
cape
dime
hat
feed

20. seat ________
21. fin ________
22. hope ________
23. bet ________
24. rob ________
25. toad ________
26. fine ________

tin
road
cob
mine
rope
get
heat

Give this a try!

Say the name of each picture. Print the vowel you hear on the line. Then circle **short** if the vowel is short. Circle **long** if it is long.

1. 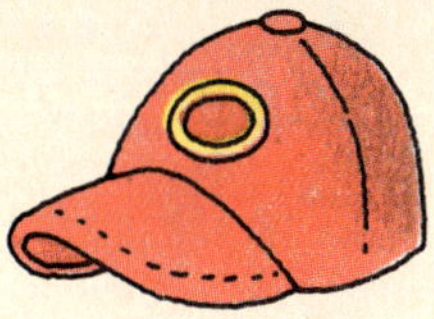
short
long

2. 
short
long

3. 
short
long

4. 
short
long

5. 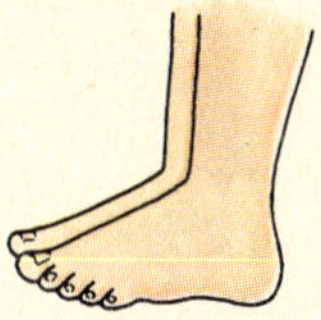
short
long

6. 
short
long

7. 
short
long

8. 
short
long

9. 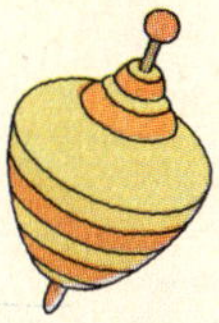
short
long

10. 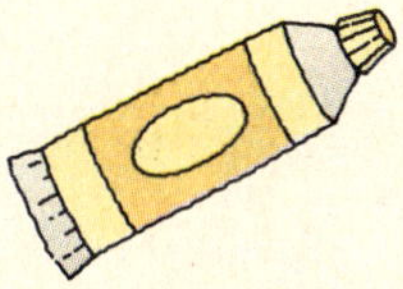
short
long

11. 
short
long

12. 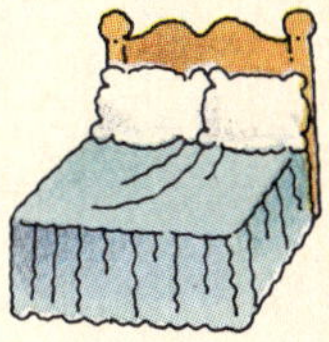
short
long

13. 
short
long

14. 
short
long

15. 
short
long

16. 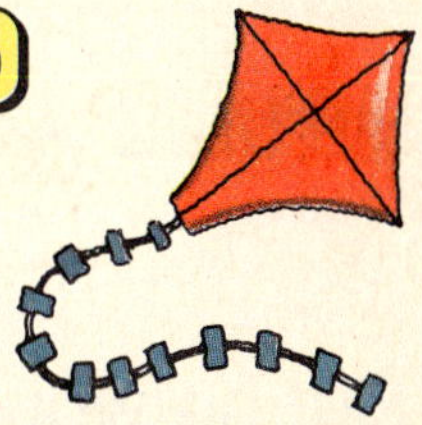
short
long

Here's what to do!

Circle the missing word for each sentence. Print it on the line.

1. I have a ____________ named Wags. fog dog day
2. His ____________ always wags. tap tape tail
3. Wags is a very ____________ dog. cute cut cat
4. He ____________ dog food by the bags. eats ears east
5. His tummy is ____________ and sags. bite big kite
6. His long ears flap ____________ flags. like lime lit
7. Wags and I like to ____________ . fat way play
8. Wags and I like to ____________ walks, too. take tack tail
9. I ____________ him to go one way. fell tell bean
10. He always ____________ the other way. toes got goes
11. But he would never ____________ away. fun run use
12. A dog like Wags is a ____________ of fun. lot lock low

Name ______________________

We went to a baseball game,
And what did we do?
Ate peanuts and popcorn and ice cream, too!

Do it this way!

Say the words in each box. Put two words together to make new words. Print the new words on the lines.

A **compound word** is made up of two or more words joined together to make a new word. **Popcorn** is corn that you pop.

1

pea	weed
sea	nut

peanut
____

2

meal	oat
my	self

____
____

3

cup	rain
coat	cake

____
____

4

be	rail
road	may

____
____

5

base	class
mate	ball

____
____

6

pack	corn
back	pop

____
____

Give this a try!

Look at the picture. Read the two words below it. Put them together to make one new word that names the picture. Print the new word on the line to finish the sentence.

1

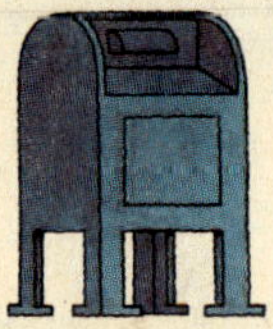

mail + box

A box for mail is a ____________________.

2

rain + coat

A coat for rain is a ____________________.

3

back + pack

A pack for your back is a ____________________.

4

sail + boat

A boat with a sail is a ____________________.

5

pop + corn

Corn that can pop is ____________________.

6

sand + box

A box full of sand is a ____________________.

7

cup + cake

A cake in a cup is a ____________________.

Name ______________________________

Off we go
to a puppet show.
So much to see
for you and me.

Here's what to do!

Say the name of each picture. Circle each vowel you hear. Print the number of syllables you hear on the line.

Many words are made of small parts called syllables.
Each syllable has one vowel sound.
go = 1 syllable   pup pet = 2 syllables

1.  2 basket
2.  ___ mittens
3. 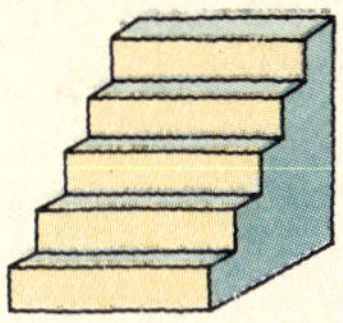 ___ steps
4.  ___ pencil
5.  ___ tent
6.  ___ puppet
7.  ___ trunk
8.  ___ robot
9. 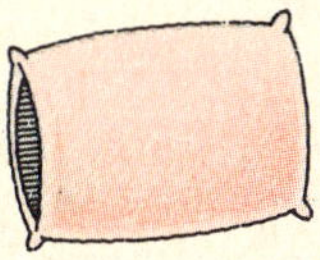 ___ pillow
10.  ___ kitten
11.  ___ tray
12.  ___ lemon

Try this!

Find the word in the box that names each picture. Print it on the line to finish the sentence.

ribbon	basket	button	pillow
kitten	boxes	seven	baby

1  Molly got a ________________ named Popcorn.

2  She put a ________________ in Popcorn's fur.

3  Popcorn was only ________________ weeks old.

4 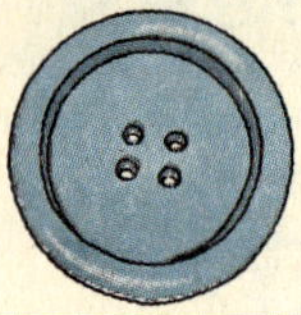 She had a nose like a ________________ .

5  She liked to play inside ________________ .

6  Molly made a bed for Popcorn in a ________________ .

7 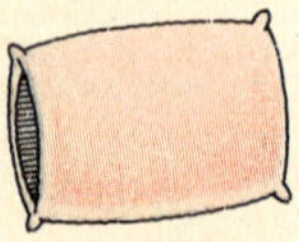 She put a ________________ in the bed to make it soft.

8  Popcorn was like a little ________________ .

Name ______________________________

Tick, tock, nine o'clock
It's time to end the day.
Tick, tock, ten o'clock
The mice come out to play!

Give this a try!

Say the name of each picture. If it has a soft **C** sound, circle the picture. If it has a hard **C** sound, color it.

When **c** is followed by **e, i,** or **y,** it usually has a soft sound. You can hear the soft **c** sound in **mice.**

1

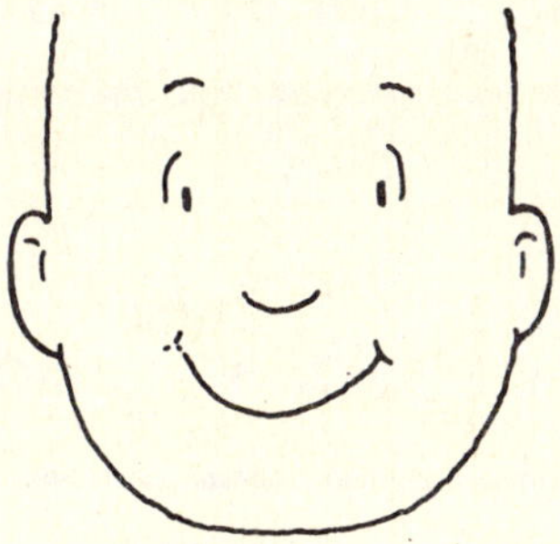

face

2

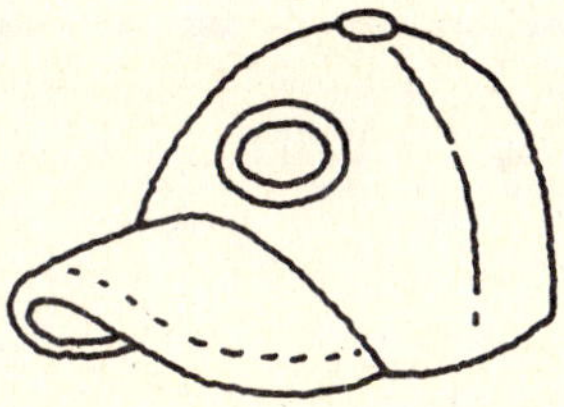

cap

3

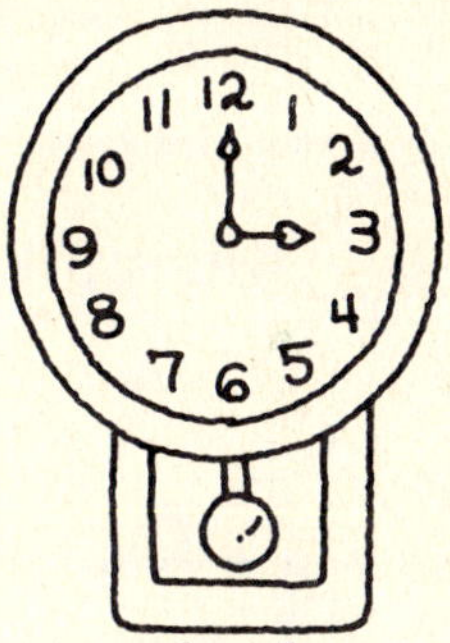

clock

4

cup

5

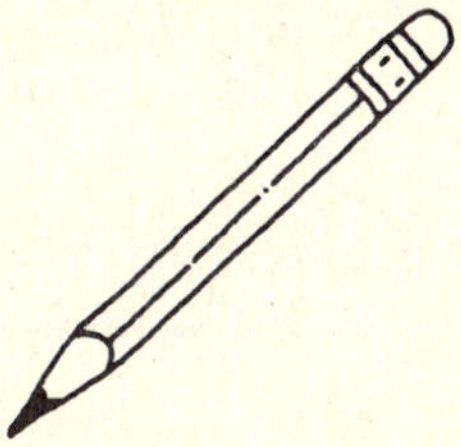

pencil

6

cake

7

mice

8

ice

9

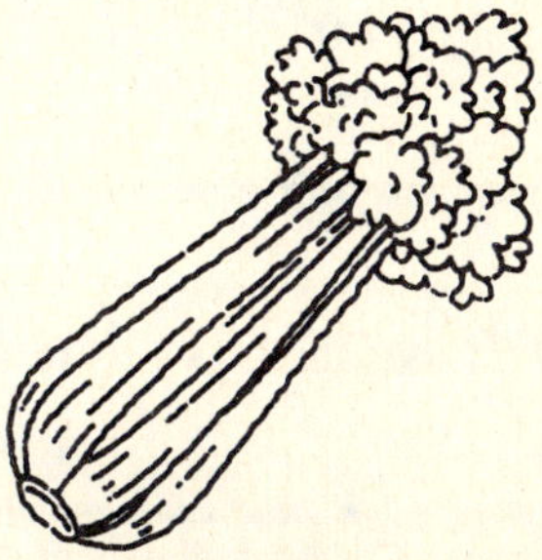

celery

Here's what to do!

Circle the word that will finish each sentence. Print it on the line.

1 Cindy and Vince ________ run fast.	can cape	cage came
2 They will run in a ________.	mice nice	race next
3 The kids ________ to watch.	cap come	cane cat
4 Cindy and Vince both hope to win first ________.	nice place	rice slice
5 They made sure the ________ of their shoes are tied.	rice laces	nice price
6 They raced to the ________.	next fence	nice celery
7 It's a tie. They both win ________ prizes.	mice nice	cereal price
8 Cindy and Vince have smiling ________.	lace race	faces space
9 The kids buy them ice cream ________.	cones mice	cape nice
10 Cindy and Vince ________ wait until the next race.	race can't	case nice

Name ______________________________

A dragon in a wagon,
A giraffe in a bath,
A goat in a coat,
They all make me laugh!

Here's what to do!

Say the name of each picture. If the name has a soft **G** sound, circle the picture. If it has a hard **G** sound, color it.

When **g** is followed by **e, i,** or **y,** it usually has a soft sound. You can hear the soft **g** sound in **giraffe.**

1

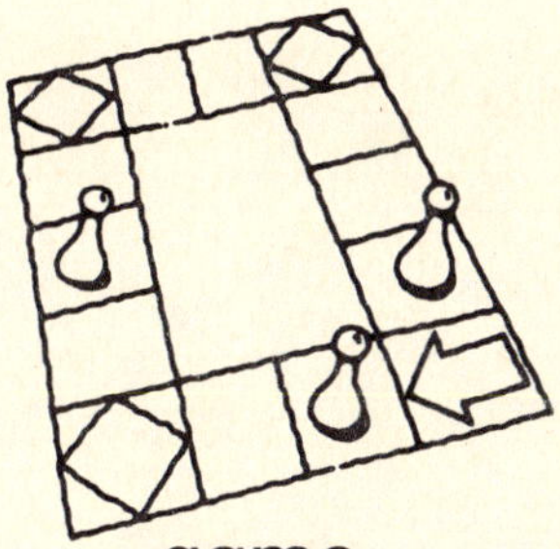

game

2

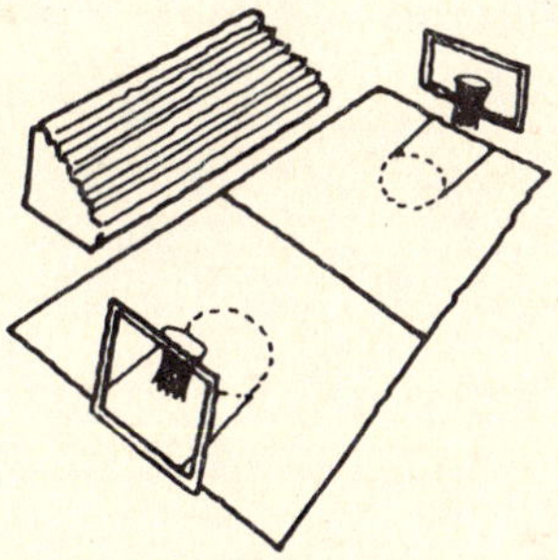

gym

3

goat

4

page

5

giant

6

gum

7

dragon

8

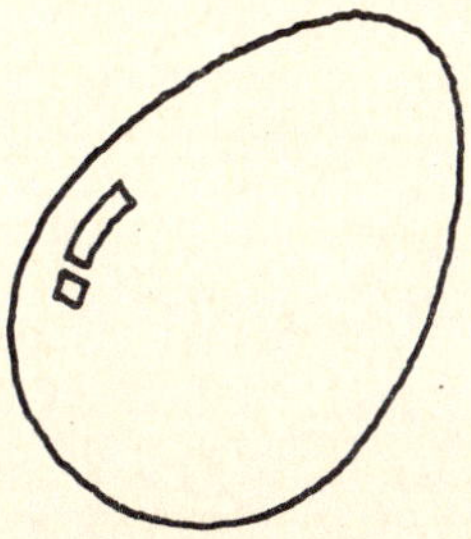

egg

9

giraffe

Do it this way!

The letter **G** can make a hard or a soft sound. Read the words in the box. Listen for the sounds of **G.** Print the words under Soft **G** or Hard **G**.

gift	gem	age	dog	cage	large
good	gum	huge	gave	goat	stage
wag	page	wage	gold	gym	gate
giant	gentle	egg	game	giraffe	give

Soft **G** words	Hard **G** words

Name ____________________

Try this!

Read the words in the box. Draw a green line under each word that has a hard **C** or **G** sound. Print each word that has a soft **C** or **G** sound on a line in a large leaf.

price
mice
goat
age
wage
games
huge
cent
gem
ice
gym
cake
race
rice
gas
cone
face
giant

Here's what to do!

Read each word. Print **S** beside each word with a soft **C** or **G** sound. Print **H** beside each word with a hard **C** or **G** sound.

1 nice ____	2 cuff ____	3 ice ____	4 cabin ____	5 lunge ____
6 camel ____	7 game ____	8 race ____	9 gull ____	10 age ____
11 came ____	12 coast ____	13 cake ____	14 coat ____	15 pencil ____
16 gym ____	17 cent ____	18 giant ____	19 gate ____	20 ridge ____
21 care ____	22 goes ____	23 recess ____	24 Vince ____	25 page ____
26 mice ____	27 rice ____	28 gem ____	29 Gail ____	30 gum ____

Now do this!

Draw a red box around each word with a soft **G** sound. Draw a blue circle around each word with a soft **C** sound.

31. A giraffe is a gentle giant.
32. You can tell by its kind face.
33. A giraffe is taller than most ceilings.
34. Giraffes think large leaves are delicious.
35. Cereal and vegetables make nice giraffe treats.
36. Zoos with giraffes need tall fences.
37. It costs money to go to the zoo in the city.
38. I need to save fifty cents more to go to the zoo.

Name ______________________________

We can be as purple as plums,
Or as green as tree frogs.
What are we?

Give this a try!

Say the name of each picture. Print its beginning blend on the line. Trace the whole word.

A **consonant blend** is two or more consonants that come together in a word. Their sounds blend together, but each sound is heard. You can hear **r** blends in **green**, **tree**, and **frogs**.

1  ____apes

2  ____og

3  ____ee

4  ____ain

Now try this!

Use the words above to answer the riddles.

5 I can jump and hop.
You find me in a pond.
I eat bugs.

I am a ______________ .

6 I am green.
You can find me in a park.
Birds live in me.

I am a ______________ .

7 I can be small or big.
I make a good toy.
I run on a track.

I am a ______________ .

8 We grow on vines.
We come in bunches.
We are good to eat.

We are ______________ .

Answer: Grapes.

Here's what to do!

Circle the word that names the picture.

1 

grapes
grass
grade

2 

trim
truck
train

3 

trade
trap
tree

4 

drive
drum
drink

5 

from
frost
fruit

6 

train
truck
trick

7 

dress
drapes
drum

8 

gray
grass
grab

Now do this!

Find the blend in each word. Circle it. Print it on the line.

9 bring ______ 10 brave ______ 11 cross ______

12 fry ______ 13 trick ______ 14 brick ______

15 trip ______ 16 grain ______ 17 trade ______

18 grade ______ 19 bride ______ 20 free ______

21 drive ______ 22 crumb ______ 23 price ______

24 grass ______ 25 train ______ 26 fruit ______

Name ____________________

What did the bee say to the flower blossom?

Give this a try!

Say the name of each picture. Print its beginning blend on the line.

1  ______

2  ______

3  ______

4 

______

5  ______

6  ______

Now try this!

Circle the word that will finish each sentence. Print it on the line.

7 Snow covers the ground like a white ______. clap cloud

8 The wind ______ the snow around. blows blue

9 It covers the trees and ______, too. plays plants

10 I like to ______ in the snow. plants play

11 I am ______ that it's wintertime. glass glad

Answer: You smell so sweet to me!

Do it this way!

Print the word on the line that answers each riddle. The pictures will help you.

1. Sometimes I ring. Sometimes I chime. I tick-tock all the time.

____

2. High up on a pole I go. With the wind I flap and blow.

____

3. I hold your food. Look for me under your hot dog.

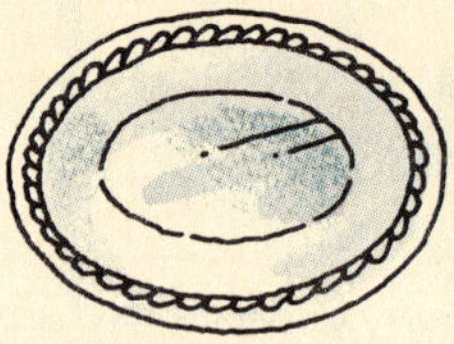

____

4. I make things stick for you. I stick to you, too.

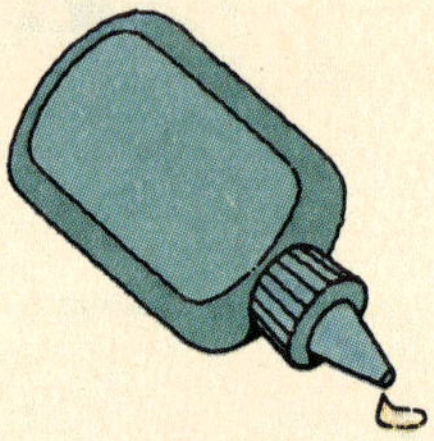

____

Now do this!

Find a word in the box to finish each sentence. Print it on the line.

5. I have a new magnifying ______________.
6. When I hold it ______________ to things they get bigger.
7. A blade of ______________ looks like a tree trunk.
8. ______________ of wood are really full of holes.
9. A ______________ looks like a big black monster!
10. A toy ______________ looks like a real plane.

Blocks
grass
fly
plane
close
glass

Name ______________________________

Here's what to do!

Say the name of each picture. Print its beginning blend on the line.

1  ______

2  ______

3 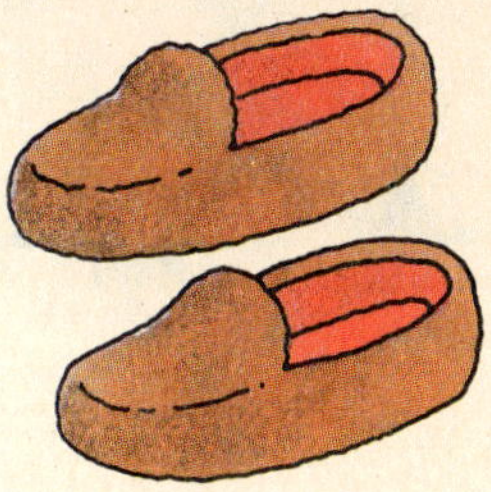 ______

4  ______

5  ______

6  ______

7  ______

8  ______

9  ______

10  ______

11  ______

12  ______

Give this a try!

Print the name of each picture on the line

1  ____

2  ____

3  ____

4  ____

Now try this!

Circle the word that will finish the sentence. Print it on the line.

5 Every day a ____ comes to my window.	from	crow	trim
6 It is big and ____ .	play	drink	black
7 I am always ____ to see my crow.	grade	glad	glass
8 It likes to get a ____ from our sprinkler.	drum	dress	drink
9 Some days I fix it a ____ of crumbs.	plate	play	plum
10 Crows like to eat bugs in the ____ .	grass	grab	grape
11 They eat bugs in ____, too.	train	trees	truck

Name ____________________

The spotted snake slid slowly down the slippery slide.

Here's what to do!

Say the name of each picture. Find its beginning blend in the box. Print it on the line.

Remember that in a **consonant blend** the sounds of the consonants blend together, but each sound is heard. You can hear **s** blends in **spotted, snake,** and **slid.**

sc	st	sp	sn	squ
scr	str	sl	sm	sw

1  ______

2  ______

3 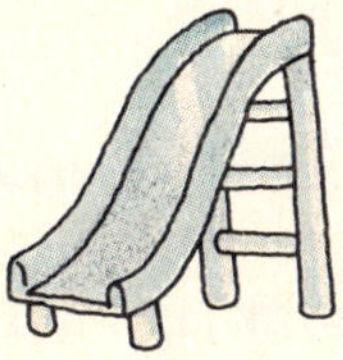 ______

4  ______

5  ______

6  ______

7  ______

8  ______

9 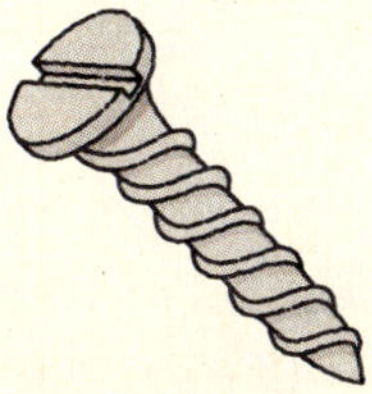 ______

10  ______

11  ______

12  ______

Do it this way!

Find a word in the box to finish each sentence. Print it on the line.

1. Did you ever ____________ to think about snakes?
2. Snakes have long, ____________ bodies.
3. Snakes can move both fast and ____________.
4. ____________ have no arms or legs.
5. They still have the ____________ to move.
6. Snakes can even ____________.
7. Their ____________ looks slimy, but it's dry.
8. Snakes ____________ some people, but not me.

scare
slim
skin
stop
skill
Snakes
swim
slow

Now do this!

Circle the name of each picture.

9. 
swim stem

10. 
scream screen

11. 
smile smoke

12. 
stops steps

13. 
snake sneak

14. 
sled slide

Name ______________________________

I like to jump,
I like to swing.
I like to run,
I like to sing.

Give this a try!

Circle the word that answers each riddle. Print it on the line.

Remember that in a **consonant blend** the sounds of the consonants blend together, but each sound is heard. You can hear blends at the end of **jump** and **sing.**

1 All mail needs these. What are they? stamps stumps ________	2 We can ride on it. What is it? string swing ________	3 An elephant has one. What is it? skunk trunk ________
4 We can eat it. What is it? toast list ________	5 It hides your face. What is it? task mask ________	6 We can sleep in it. What is it? tent plant ________
7 We have two of these. What are they? lands hands ________	8 Fish swim in it. What is it? tank wink ________	9 It can float. What is it? raft left ________

Here's what to do!

Find the word in the box that names each picture. Print it on the line.

milk	skunk	tent	belt	trunk	plants
nest	ring	stamp	raft	desk	tusk

1

____

2
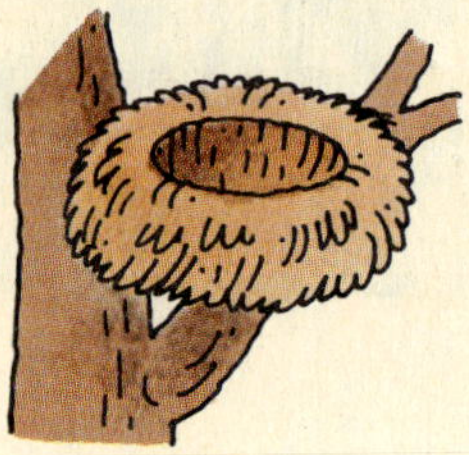
____

3

____

4
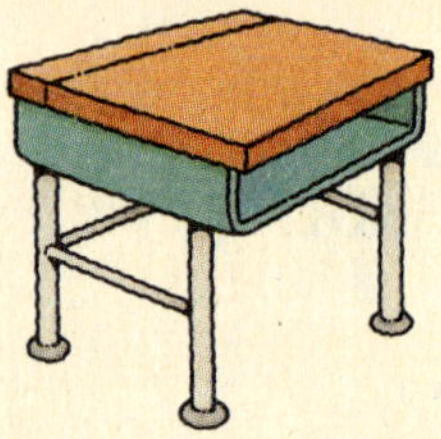
____

5

____

6

____

7
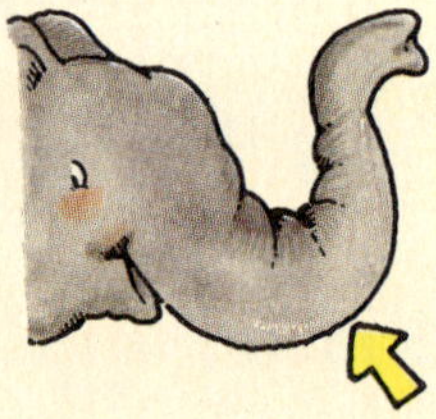
____

8

____

9

____

10
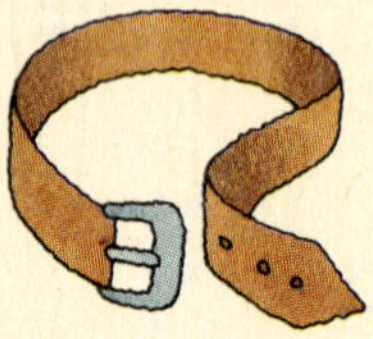
____

11
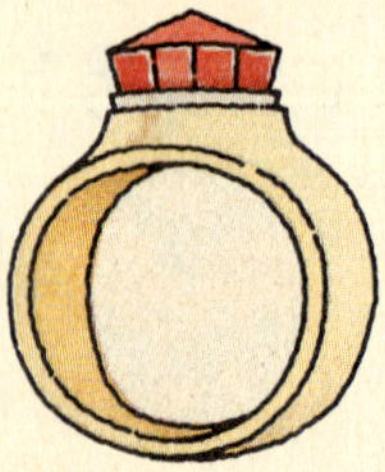
____

12

____

Name ______________________________

Try this!

Find the missing word for each sentence by changing the blend of the word beside it to make a new word. Print it on the line. Use the blends in the box to help you.

sk	sp	tr	dr	str	br
fr	gl	sl	fl	pl	bl

1. I went to ______________. — creep
2. I had a strange ______________. — scream
3. The grass changed from green to ______________. — clown
4. The ______________ was full of cows saying, "Boo!" — sleet
5. A ______________ was full of cotton candy. — free
6. It ______________ in the wind. — flew
7. A big green ______________ went flying past me. — slog
8. I jumped out of bed in a ______________. — crash
9. My ______________ had goose bumps. — spin
10. My head was in a ______________. — grin
11. I dumped a ______________ of water on top of me. — class
12. The dream did ______________ tricks on me. — clay

Here's what to do!

Circle the blend that will complete the word in the sentence. Print the blend on the line. Trace the whole word.

1. I liked to play with my ______ain______. fr br tr

2. We like to climb ______ees______. tr fr br

3. Sometimes we ______im______ in the pool. cr sc sw

4. Sometimes we fish in a ______eam______. str fr tr

5. We like to ______end______ time together. sp sm sn

Now do this!

Find a word in the box to finish each sentence. Print it on the line.

small
swim
frog
stream
floated
climbed

6. We saw a green ____________.

7. It was very ____________.

8. The frog ____________ up onto a lily pad.

9. The lily pad ____________ on a stream.

10. The ____________ flowed through the woods.

11. Soon the frog jumped in the stream for a ____________.

Name ____________________

See my little cherry tree,
With a rosy cherry just for me.
Won't you try my tasty treat?
A better snack you'll never eat!

Give this a try!

Circle each word in which **Y** has a long **E** sound.

Sometimes **y** can stand for the vowel sound of long **e** or long **i**. You can hear the long **e** sound in **cherry.**

baby	cry	happy	why
try	every	hurry	tiny
Molly	sandy	shy	puppy
penny	Freddy	funny	bunny

Now try this!

Circle the words in the sentences in which **Y** has a long **E** sound.

1. Ty and Molly were helping take care of baby Freddy.
2. They heard Freddy cry in his crib.
3. They went to help in a hurry.
4. They had to try everything to make him happy.
5. Ty read him a funny book about fish that fly.
6. Molly gave him her bunny to play with.
7. Ty made very silly faces.
8. Finally Freddy was happy.

Here's what to do!

Circle each word with a **Y** that sounds like long **I.**

When **y** is the only vowel at the end of a one-syllable word, **y** usually has the long **i** sound. You can hear the long **i** sound in **try.**

try	Freddy	sly	buggy	funny
bunny	dry	silly	rocky	my
Ty	windy	by	sky	sunny
sleepy	fly	happy	muddy	cry
sneaky	lucky	shy	puppy	Molly
why	jolly	baby	fry	very

Now do this!

Circle each word with **Y** that sounds like long **I** in the sentences.

1. Why do onions make us cry when we are happy?
2. Why is the sky blue on a sunny day?
3. Why do bats fly at night?
4. Why is a desert dry and a swamp muddy?
5. Why can a bird fly but not a puppy?
6. Why do we look silly if we try to fly?
7. Why is a fox sneaky and sly?
8. Why is a bunny shy?
9. Why does a rainy sky make you sleepy?
10. Do you ever wonder why?

Name ____________________

Try this!

Read the word in each paw print. If the **Y** stands for a long **I** sound, color it yellow. If it stands for a long **E** sound, color it orange.

cry | bunny | sorry | my | Yuppy

try | why | shy | sunny | any

Now try this!

Find a word from the top of the page to finish each sentence. Print it on the line.

1. ____________ the puppy was digging a hole.
2. Suddenly he heard a ____________ from inside.
3. A very angry ____________ popped out of the hole.
4. "Why are you digging up ____________ happy home?"
5. Yuppy yapped, "Oh, my! I'm very ____________."
6. "I'll ____________ to help you fix it up!"

Here's what to do!

Say the name of each picture. Circle each word that has the same sound of **Y** as the picture name.

1

baby
my
fly
fifty
funny

2

sky
sunny
fairy
cry
Bobby

3

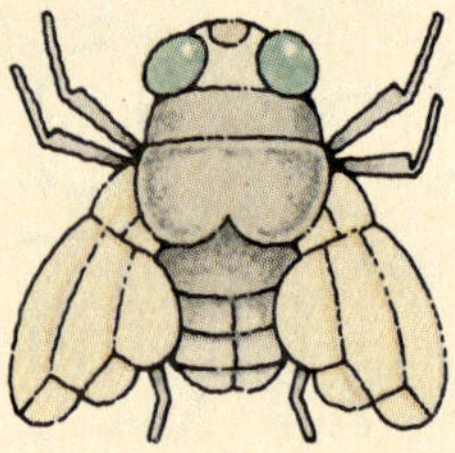

dolly
try
sly
kitty
dry

4

lady
penny
shy
fry
happy

5

why
silly
lily
by
bunny

6

my
sixty
fly
Sally
sky

7

jelly
Sandy
my
fry
cry

8

lucky
try
fifty
sky
puppy

9

berry
very
try
sly
any

10

cry
lady
many
sky
by

11

only
city
July
spy
funny

12

my
fly
fifty
happy
silly

Name ______________________________

When sitting in her chair each night,
Beth sees the stars shining so bright.

Do it this way!

Circle the word that will finish each sentence. Print it on the line.

A **consonant digraph** is two consonants that together stand for one sound. You can hear consonant digraphs in **when, chair, the,** and **shine.**

1. I go to the zoo to see the ______________.	chop	chimp	check
2. It smiles to show its ______________.	then	teeth	these
3. They are big and ______________.	which	what	white
4. It eats bananas by the ______________.	bunch	reach	much
5. Once I saw it eat a ______________.	that	ship	peach
6. Sometimes it dumps its ______________.	wish	dish	swish
7. Then it naps in the ______________.	fresh	shut	shade

Now do this!

Find two words from the top of the page that begin with **ch, wh, th,** and **sh**. Print them on the lines beside the correct consonant digraph.

8. ______________ ch ______________	9. ______________ th ______________
10. ______________ wh ______________	11. ______________ sh ______________

Do it this way!

Fill in the bubble beside the word that will finish each sentence. Print it on the line.

1. Chip and I didn't know ______________ to go. ○ where ○ what
2. We decided to go to the mall to ______________. ○ chop ○ shop
3. They sell everything ______________. ○ this ○ there
4. There was so ______________ to choose from. ○ catch ○ much
5. I couldn't decide ______________ I wanted most. ○ what ○ who
6. Then I saw some model ______________ kits. ○ shirt ○ ship
7. ______________ was what I wanted most. ○ When ○ That
8. I ______________ a clipper ship to make. ○ chose ○ chair
9. ______________ chose a spaceship kit. ○ Choose ○ Chip
10. ______________ we had lunch. ○ Then ○ That
11. A little ______________ later, we went home. ○ while ○ what
12. I put together my ship ______________ night. ○ then ○ that

Name ______________________________

Give this a try!

Say each word in the box. If the consonant digraph is at the beginning of a word, print the word in the first column. If it is in the middle, print the word in the second column. If it is at the end, print the word in the third column.

cheer	quack	thank	stuck	while	teacher	brother
when	father	kicking	peach	dishes	cracker	what
bath	wishing	fish	thin	beach	why	wash
chin	clothes	shell	touch	mother	reach	

Beginning	Middle	End

Try this!

Say the name of each picture. Circle the consonant digraph you hear.

1

th
sh
ck
ch
wh

2

th
sh
ck
ch
wh

3

th
sh
ck
ch
wh

4

th
sh
ck
ch
wh

5

th
sh
ck
ch
wh

6
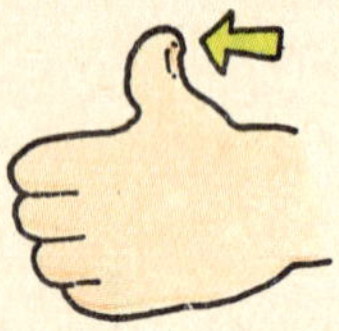
th
sh
ck
ch
wh

7
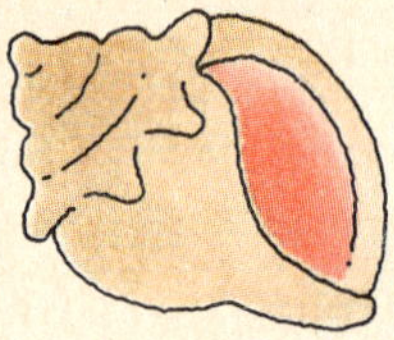
th
sh
ck
ch
wh

8

th
sh
ck
ch
wh

9

th
sh
ck
ch
wh

10

th
sh
ck
ch
wh

11

th
sh
ck
ch
wh

12

th
sh
ck
ch
wh

13

th
sh
ck
ch
wh

14

th
sh
ck
ch
wh

15
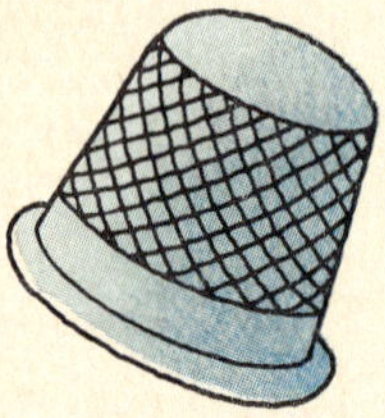
th
sh
ck
ch
wh

16

th
sh
ck
ch
wh

Name ______________________________

Who is in that suit you see?
It's a knight with knocking knees.

Give this a try!

Read each sentence. Find the picture it tells about. Write the sentence letter under the picture.

You can hear the consonant digraph **kn** in **knight, knocking,** and **knees.**

1

a. John has a knot in the rope.
b. I know what is in the box.
c. Joan turned the knob.

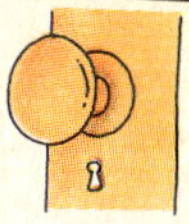

2

a. Theo will knock down the pile.
b. Mom cut it with a knife.
c. Joe knocks on the door.

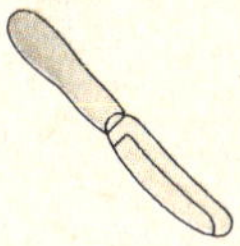

3

a. The knight wore armor.
b. Tad's knee needs a patch.
c. Grandma likes to knit.

Now try this!

Find a word in the box that answers each riddle. Print it on the line.

4 Something that can cut. ____________

5 Someone who wore armor. ____________

6 Something you can tie. ____________

knife
knot
knight

Here's what to do!

Circle the word that will finish each sentence. Print it on the line.

1. I ______________ how to do many things. know knot
2. I can spread butter with a ______________. knot knife
3. I can touch my ______________ to my chin. knees knew
4. I can tie ______________. knots knits
5. I can turn a door ______________. knee knob
6. I can read about ______________. know knights
7. I can ______________ a sweater. knit knife
8. I've ______________ how to do these things for a long time. knit known

Now do this!

Think of a word that begins with **kn** and rhymes with each word. Print it on the line.

9. snow ______	10. block ______	11. wife ______
12. blew ______	13. see ______	14. hot ______
15. own ______	16. sit ______	17. sob ______

Name ______________________________

Can you whistle?
I can, too.
Listen now
And I'll whistle for you.

Here's what to do!

Find the name of each picture in the box. Print it on the line.

apple	eagle	people
candle	buckle	whistle
turtle	bottle	table

1 

____

2 

____

3 

____

4 

____

5 

____

6 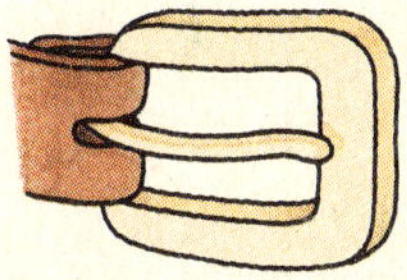

____

7 

____

8 

____

9 

____

Do it this way!

Find the word that will finish each sentence. Print it on the line.

1. A ______________ uses its own shell for a house.
2. It can swim in a small ______________.
3. It can ______________ around in the puddle.
4. It can climb on rocks and ______________.
5. An ______________ might fly over and scare it.
6. Sometimes ______________ may scare it, too.
7. Then the turtle can ______________ safely in its shell.

pebbles
eagle
people
turtle
huddle
puddle
paddle

---

8. I have a ______________ pet turtle.
9. My ______________ gave it to me.
10. It's not even as big as a ______________.
11. I named my turtle ______________.
12. When I hold it, its feet ______________ my hand.
13. Then I laugh and ______________.
14. Sometimes, it sits on the ______________ next to my bed.

giggle
table
little
Wiggle
pickle
tickle
uncle

Name ______________________________

I wrote a poem yesterday
About the fun on my birthday.
I got a great big gift, you know,
that was all wrapped up with a bow.

Give this a try!

Find the word in the box that will finish each sentence. Print it on the line.

You can hear the consonant digraph **wr** in **wrote** and **wrapped.**

wren	wreck	wrap	wrestle	write
wrist	wrench	wrecker	wrong	wriggle

1. To move around is to ______________.
2. The opposite of **right** is ______________.
3. A small bird is a ______________.
4. A thing that is ruined is a ______________.
5. To hide a gift in paper is to ______________ it.
6. When you put a story on paper you ______________.
7. Your ______________ holds your hand to your arm.
8. A truck that clears away wrecks is a ______________.
9. A kind of tool is a ______________.
10. One way to fight is to ______________.

Here's what to do!

Find a word in the box that answers each riddle. Print it on the line.

wren	wrecker	wriggle	wrap	wrist
wrench	wreath	writer	typewriter	wrinkle

1. I am round and pretty.
You can hang me up.
What am I?

____

2. I hide a gift.
You tear me up.
What am I?

____

3. I can fly.
I like to sing.
What am I?

____

4. I am a useful tool.
I can fix things.
What am I?

____

5. I am next to a hand.
I can twist and bend.
What am I?

____

6. I can print.
People press my keys.
What am I?

____

7. I am a big truck.
I tow things away.
What am I?

____

8. I write stories. They can be real or make believe.
What am I?

____

9. I am a fold in a dress.
I am a crease in a face.
What am I?

____

10. I am another word for **squirm**.
I rhyme with **giggle**.
What am I?

____

Name ______________________________

Do it this way!

Find the word in the box that will finish each sentence. Print it on the line.

knocked
know
knuckles
Knights
write
wriggled
wrapped
written
knees
wrecked
knew

1. I like to read stories ______________ about knights.

2. ______________ lived a long time ago.

3. They ______________ themselves in metal armor.

4. It was the only way they ______________ to protect themselves.

5. Armor gloves protected the knights' hands and ______________.

6. The legs of the armor bent at the ______________.

7. I'd like to ______________ more about wearing armor.

8. Did metal armor ever get ______________?

9. Could a knight get up if he were ______________ off a horse?

10. I wonder if knights ______________ inside their armor!

11. I'll find out all I can and ______________ a report about it.

Try this!

Say the name of each picture. Print the consonant digraphs where you hear them in the words. Some words will have two consonant digraphs.

1

2
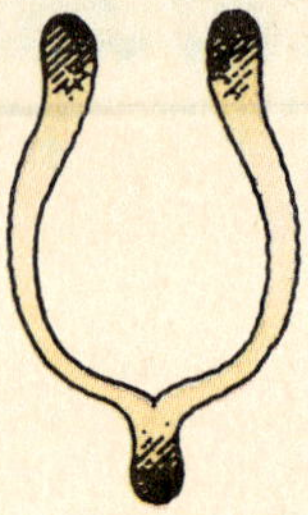

3

4

5

6

7

8

9

10

11

12

Name ____________________

Give this a try!

Find the word that answers each riddle. Print its letter on the line.

1	A bike rolls on them.	____	a. sheep
2	It gives us wool.	____	b. brush
3	It is something we use for our hair.	____	c. whale
4	It can blow air and water from a hole in its head.	____	d. wheels
5	This is used to cut things.	____	e. knife

6	We use a pencil to do this.	____	a. teeth
7	It is not fair to do this.	____	b. rattle
8	This is a chair fit for a king.	____	c. cheat
9	These show when we smile.	____	d. throne
10	Wind makes a door do this.	____	e. write

11	These are fun to find on the beach.	____	a. whisper
12	These taste good.	____	b. peaches
13	This is a quiet way to talk.	____	c. shells
14	Smoke goes up this.	____	d. clock
15	This tells us the time.	____	e. chimney

Now try this!

Say the name of each picture. Print its missing letters on the line. Trace the whole word.

1. 

eese

2. 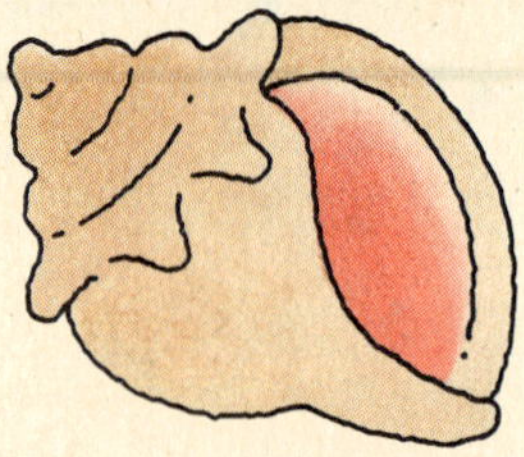

ell

3. 

app

4. 

ock

5. 

ite

6. 

tru

7. 

di es

8. 

cand

9. 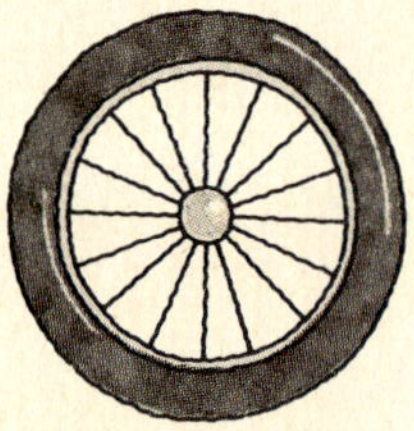

eel

10. 

turt

11. 

irty

12. 

erry

Name ____

On the farm, in a barn,
Animals live safe from harm.

Here's what to do!

Find the word in the box that will finish each sentence. Print it on the line.

An **r** after a vowel makes the vowel have a sound that is different from the usual short or long sound. You can hear the **ar** sound in **barn, farm,** and **harm**.

apart	star	hard
part	car	hardly
start	large	jars

1. I picked out a new model ______________ kit.
2. I got two ______________ of paint, too.
3. I could hardly wait to ______________ on it.
4. I glued it so the car wouldn't fall ______________ .
5. There were small parts and ______________ parts.
6. The tires were ______________ to fit, but I did it.
7. I stuck gold ______________ stickers on the sides.
8. I could ______________ believe it when it was done.
9. The best ______________ was showing it to my friends.

Do it this way!

Finish each sentence. Use a word that rhymes with the word beside the sentence. Print it on the line.

1. A shark is a very ______________ animal. — part
2. It lives in the deep, ______________ part of the ocean. — bark
3. It can grow to be very ______________. — barge
4. A shark's teeth are very ______________. — carp
5. It has no problem tearing food ______________. — start
6. I live ______________ from the ocean where sharks live. — star
7. I like to visit the animal ______________. — lark
8. It's not ______________ from my house. — car
9. I can watch the sharks there free from ______________. — farm

Now do this!

Print three rhyming words under each word.

10 mark	11 start	12 hard
______________	______________	______________
______________	______________	______________
______________	______________	______________

Name ______________________________

My ears are good for you to eat,
with a fork or in your hands.
What am I?

Here's what to do!

Read each riddle. Answer it with a word that rhymes with the word beside the riddle. Print it on the line.

Remember that an **r** after a vowel makes the vowel have a sound that is different from the usual short or long sound. You can hear the **or** sound in **for** and **fork.**

1 Something we can pop and eat.	______________	horn
2 Something on a unicorn.	______________	born
3 Something we eat with.	______________	cork
4 Something with rain, wind, and thunder.	______________	form
5 Something we can play or watch.	______________	port
6 Something sharp on a rose.	______________	born
7 Something beside the sea.	______________	tore
8 Something to close up a bottle.	______________	pork
9 Something that gives us light.	______________	porch

Answer: Corn.

Now try this!

Circle the name of each picture.

1

home
horse
horn

2

arm
are
am

3

barn
bark
book

4

home
horse
horn

5

fifty
forty
fairy

6

torch
tar
scorch

7

car
card
cost

8

come
corn
cart

9

store
stand
star

10

horn
thirty
thorn

11

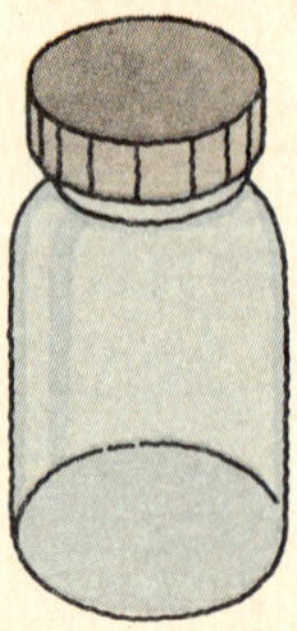

car
jar
jam

12

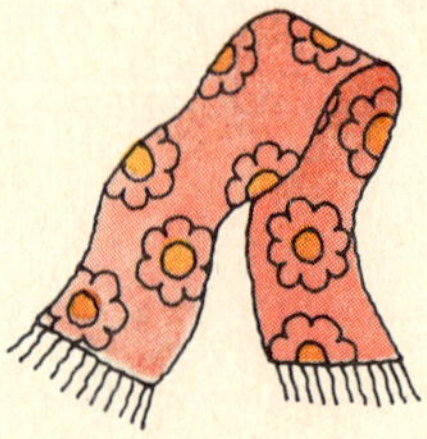

scarf
scare
scorn

Sparky the Shark

This book belongs to

_______________________________. 1

Sparky's mother tried to teach him.
"Stay in this part of the sea," she said.
"Don't swim too close to the shore." 3

The force of the storm drove Sparky onto a sand bar.
When the storm ended, Sparky was worn out.
6 He was far, far from home.

Print what Sparky and his mother said to each other after she brought him
8 home.

FOLD

FOLD

Sparky the shark was born in a large harbor.
He never swam far from his mother.

2

As Sparky got older, he forgot her warning.
He swam off to explore.
He swam toward the shore.

4

Just then, a horrible storm began.
The sea grew dark.
Sparky was tossed around like a cork on the waves.

5

Sparky's mother found him and led him home.
Sparky never forgot the storm.
He stayed close to his mother forever more.

7

FOLD

FOLD

Name ______________________________

It's sometimes shaped liked a circle.
It's the home of a turtle and other animals.
What is it?

Give this a try!

Circle each word that has the same vowel sound as the name of the picture.

Remember that an **r** after a vowel makes the vowel have a sound that is different from the usual short or long sound. You can hear the **ir** sound in **circle,** the **ur** sound in **turtle,** and the **er** sound in **other.**

1 ir

bird

first
fork
skirt
shirt
girl

2 ur

turtle

curb
purse
card
nurse
fur

3 er

fern

batter
letter
hammer
park
clerk

Now try this!

Find the name of each picture in the words above. Print each name on the lines.

4  ______

5  ______

6  ______

7  ______

8  ______

9  ______

10  ______

11 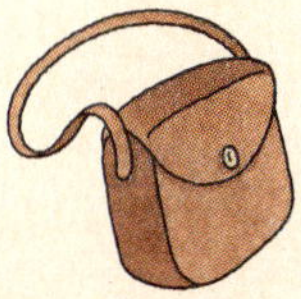 ______

Answer: A shell.

Do it this way!

Circle the name of the picture. Color the box with the same vowel with **r.**

1 

bird
barn
burn

er	or	ir

2 

first
batter
farm

ir	er	ar

3 

tar
turtle
third

ur	ar	or

4 

hammer
farmer
summer

ir	or	er

5 

shirt
skirt
scarf

ar	ir	ur

6 

goat
garden
girl

ir	or	ur

Now do this!

Circle the word that will finish the sentence. Print it on the line.

7 Cats have ______________ and purr. far fur

8 Birds have feathers and ______________. cheat chirp

9 Turtles ______________ up inside their shells. curl car

10 Fish have fins and swim in the ______________. river hurt

11 Worms wiggle and live in ______________. burn dirt

12 Have you ______________ wondered why? other ever

Name ______________________________

Here's what to do!

Find the vowel followed by **r** in each word. Print the two letters on the line. Then print the number of the picture with the same two letters.

1 car	2 horn	3 bird	4 hammer	5 turtle

1 part	______	___	12 chirp	______	___
2 verse	______	___	13 park	______	___
3 turn	______	___	14 horse	______	___
4 pork	______	___	15 fur	______	___
5 first	______	___	16 skirt	______	___
6 party	______	___	17 curb	______	___
7 third	______	___	18 short	______	___
8 bark	______	___	19 purse	______	___
9 fern	______	___	20 under	______	___
10 storm	______	___	21 hard	______	___
11 her	______	___	22 burn	______	___

Give this a try!

Circle the letters that will finish the word in each sentence. Print them on the line. Trace the whole word.

1. Many different things happen in sp ____ ts. er or ir
2. A diver jumps in the water head f ____ st. ur ir ar
3. A s ____ fer stands up on the ocean waves. ar or ur
4. A ski jump ____ glides off high cliffs. ir er ur
5. There ____ e ____ some sports I like to play. or er ar
6. There are oth ____ I'd rather watch. ar ir er
7. Socc ____ is a game I like to play. ir ur er
8. Tennis is a game I'd rath ____ watch. ar or er

Now try this!

Use the words in the box to answer the riddles.

bark	skirt	car	park	fur	corn

9. It is part of a dress. ____
10. You like to eat it. ____
11. Dogs make this noise. ____
12. A rabbit has it. ____
13. A person can drive it. ____
14. We play games in it. ____

Name ____________________

Here's what to do!

Say the name of each picture. Fill in the bubble beside its vowel with **r.**

1

○ ur
○ or
○ ar

2

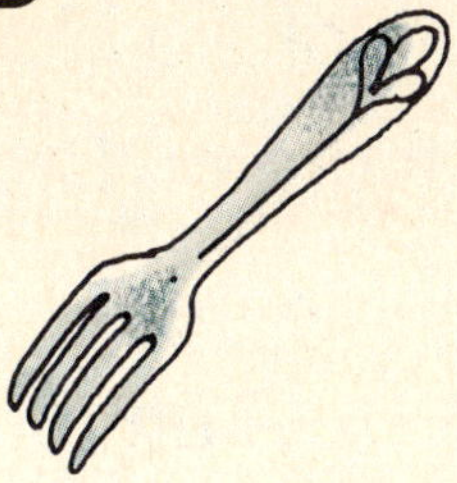

○ ar
○ er
○ or

3

○ ar
○ er
○ or

4

○ er
○ or
○ ar

5

○ ar
○ er
○ or

6

○ or
○ ar
○ ir

7

○ ar
○ or
○ ir

8

○ or
○ ur
○ ar

9

○ ir
○ or
○ ar

10

○ or
○ ur
○ ar

11

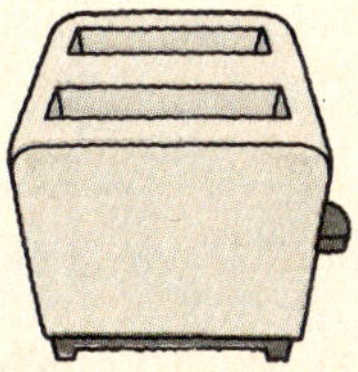

○ er
○ ar
○ or

12

○ ur
○ or
○ ar

Here's what to do!

Draw a line under each word in the sentences with **ar, or, ir, er,** or **ur.** Then do what each sentence tells you to do.

1. Do you see the skirt? Circle the skirt. Color the skirt purple.
2. See the letter. Color it green. Make a black dot near it.
3. Can you see the fern? Color it green. Draw a line under it.
4. Find the turkey. Color its feathers orange and yellow.
5. See the barn. Make a little black **X** under it. Color the barn red.
6. Do you see the corn. Color the corn yellow. Draw a box around it.
7. See the star. Color it blue. Make two red dots near the star.
8. Look at the turtle. Make a blue **X** under it. Color it green and black.
9. Find the horse. Draw a line under it. Color the horse brown.
10. See the car. Draw a circle around it. Color it blue.

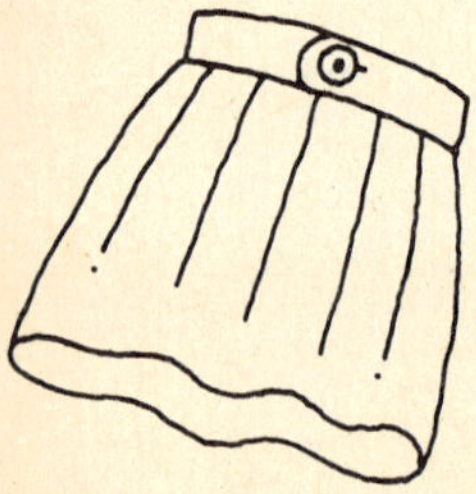

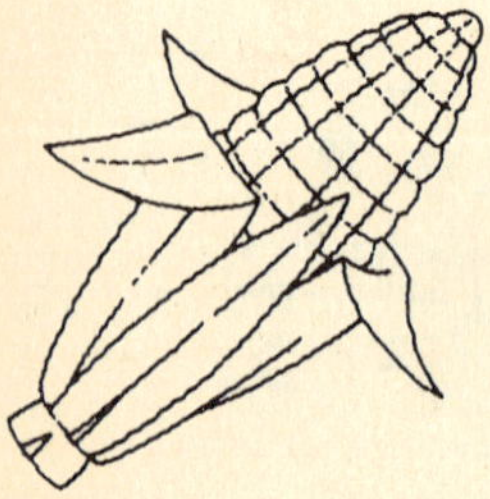

The Barn in Winter

This book belongs to

________________________. 1

The farmer's herd of cows are in the barn.
The farm horses stay warm in the barn, too.

3

6 The mice have a nest in a dark corner.
They hurry and scurry and gather corn to eat.

8 What is winter like where you live?
Write a few sentences that tell about it.

FOLD

FOLD

In Vermont, winter days are short.
Stormy winds are sharp and cold.
Who lives in this barn during the
winter?

2

The barn cat sleeps in the corner.
She looks like a ball of fur.
Is she dreaming of warm weather?

7

FOLD

Turkeys and chickens live in part of
the barn.
They don't mind the horses and cows
nearby.

4

Birds perch on beams high in the barn.
They fly in circles stirring up dirt.

5

FOLD

Name ____________________

He'll get the broom,
then we'll clean our room.

Do it this way!

Print a word from the box that means the same as the two words beside each line.

A **contraction** is a short way of writing two words. It is formed by putting two words together and leaving out one or more letters. An apostrophe (') is used to show where something is left out. Some contractions are formed with the word **will.**

we will = we'll

you'll	they'll	she'll
we'll	I'll	he'll

1. I will ____________
2. he will ____________
3. we will ____________
4. they will ____________
5. she will ____________
6. you will ____________

Now do this!

Print the short form of the two underlined words in each sentence.

7. <u>I will</u> get in the boat and you'll get in, too. ____________
8. <u>He will</u> climb aboard. ____________
9. <u>She will</u> join us and jump in. ____________
10. <u>They will</u> hop in for the ride. ____________
11. All aboard? Oh, no! <u>We will</u> sink! ____________

Give this a try!

Print a word from the box that means the same as the two words beside each line.

Some contractions are formed with the word **not.**
does not = doesn't

can't	couldn't	weren't	doesn't	don't
didn't	aren't	isn't	won't	haven't

1. are not ______
2. do not ______
3. did not ______
4. will not ______
5. were not ______
6. is not ______
7. could not ______
8. can not ______
9. does not ______
10. have not ______

Now try this!

Print two words that mean the same as each underlined word.

11. Mitten the kitten <u>can't</u> get down from the tree. ______
12. She <u>isn't</u> brave enough to climb down. ______
13. She <u>doesn't</u> know what to do. ______
14. We <u>haven't</u> any problem getting her down. ______
15. "<u>Aren't</u> you a lucky kitten to have friends to help?" ______

Name ______________________________

Do it this way!

Circle two words in each sentence that can be made into one of the contractions in the box. Print the contraction on the line.

Some contractions are formed with the word **is.**
he is = he's

he is = he's	That is = That's	it is = it's
she is = she's	It is = It's	

1. It is Rocky's birthday. ______________

2. What a surprise he is going to get! ______________

3. Jess has his gift, but she is hiding it. ______________

4. Do you think it is something Rocky wants? ______________

5. What will Rocky get? Look at the picture at the top. That is what Rocky wants the most. ______________

Here's what to do!

Print the contraction that means the same as the underlined words in each sentence.

Some contractions are formed with the word **have.**

You have = You've
I have = I've
We have = We've
They have = They've

1

I have made you smile.

________________ made you smile.

2

We have shown you tricks.

________________ shown you tricks.

3

They have tossed a ball with their noses.

________________ tossed a ball with their noses.

4

You have had a good time.

________________ had a good time.

Name ____________________

Give this a try!

Print two words that mean the same as the underlined word in each sentence.

Contractions can be formed using the words **am, are,** or **us.**

I am = I'm
we are = we're
let us = let's

1. Let's have a party. ____________
2. We'll ask our friends to come. ____________
3. I'm going to pop popcorn. ____________
4. He's going to bring some lemonade. ____________
5. She's going to bring some cupcakes. ____________
6. They're going to bring games. ____________
7. We're going to have fun! ____________

Now try this!

Print the contraction that means the same as the two words beside the line.

8. you are ____________
9. she is ____________
10. I am ____________
11. it is ____________
12. let us ____________
13. they are ____________
14. we are ____________
15. we will ____________
16. he is ____________
17. they will ____________
18. I will ____________
19. he will ____________

Here's what to do!

Print the letter of each contraction next to the words that have the same meaning.

a. we're	**b.** you'll	**c.** it's	**d.** can't	**e.** I'm
f. he's	**g.** won't	**h.** let's	**i.** don't	**j.** she's
k. you're	**l.** isn't	**m.** he'll	**n.** we'll	**o.** I'll
p. I've	**q.** they'll	**r.** she'll	**s.** we've	**t.** aren't

1 _____ I am	**2** _____ we are	**3** _____ will not	**4** _____ he is
5 _____ you will	**6** _____ let us	**7** _____ can not	**8** _____ it is
9 _____ is not	**10** _____ you are	**11** _____ I will	**12** _____ we will
13 _____ do not	**14** _____ I have	**15** _____ she will	**16** _____ she is
17 _____ he will	**18** _____ we have	**19** _____ are not	**20** _____ they will

Now do this!

Find a word in the box that will finish each sentence. Print it on the line.

Let's
I'm
It's
I'll
don't
we're

21 ______________ go skating in the park.

22 ______________ time for us to go.

23 I ______________ want to be late.

24 I know ______________ ready now, are you?

25 ______________ help you find your skates.

26 I think ______________ going to have fun.

Name ______________________________

Give this a try!

Print two words that mean the same as each contraction.

1. I've ______________
2. didn't ______________
3. he'll ______________
4. they've ______________
5. you're ______________
6. let's ______________
7. isn't ______________
8. won't ______________
9. haven't ______________
10. I'll ______________
11. hasn't ______________
12. they're ______________
13. you'll ______________
14. I'm ______________

Now try this!

Print the contraction for the underlined words in each sentence.

15. I <u>have not</u> heard Jake's story yet. ______________
16. He <u>has not</u> read it aloud. ______________
17. I <u>can not</u> wait to hear it. ______________
18. Now <u>he will</u> read his story to the class. ______________
19. <u>Let us</u> listen to him. ______________
20. <u>You are</u> a good reader, Jake. ______________
21. <u>I will</u> help you make a book from your story. ______________

Do it this way!

Print the contraction for the two words beside each line.

1. I have ______
2. can not ______
3. do not ______
4. that is ______
5. let us ______
6. there is ______
7. did not ______
8. you have ______
9. she is ______
10. could not ______

Now do this!

Circle the contraction that will finish each sentence. Print it on the line.

11. ______ a surprise for Linda. Didn't It's
12. ______ her new bike. That's Isn't
13. She ______ guess what it is. won't you're
14. She ______ think she'll get one. aren't doesn't
15. ______ here now! She's You'll
16. "Linda, ______ going to show you something." we're don't
17. "______ be very surprised!" There's You'll

Name ______________________________

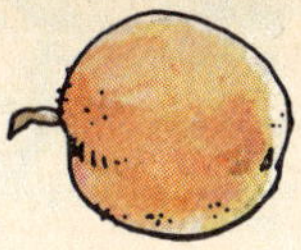

I'll have one peach for lunch.

Here are some peaches for my pals to munch.

Here's what to do!

Circle the word that will finish each sentence. Print it on the line. Color one or more pictures in each box to match the answer.

When **s** or **es** is added to a word it forms the plural. Plural means "more than one." If a word ends in **x, z, ss, sh,** or **ch,** usually add **es** to make it mean more than one. For other words just add **s.**

one dish, two dish**es**
one dress, many dress**es**
one chick, three chick**s**

1. At the zoo we saw some
   seal   seals

   ______________________ .

2. We like to eat fresh
   peach   peaches

   ______________________ .

3. We have toys in three
   box   boxes
   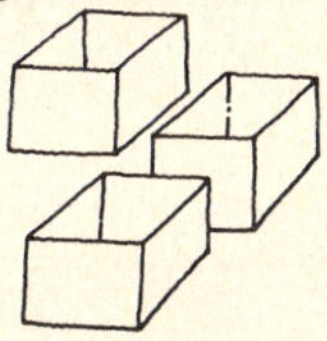
   ______________________ .

4. June will use a hair
   brush   brushes
   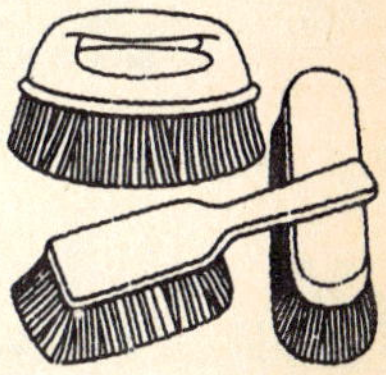
   ______________________ .

5. Ed's mom gave him a
   cap   caps
   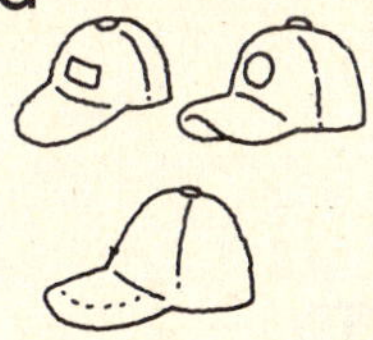
   ______________________ .

6. Just look at those
   dog   dogs

   ______________________ .

7. Look at those shiny
   star   stars

   ______________________ .

8. The box was used for
   mitten   mittens
   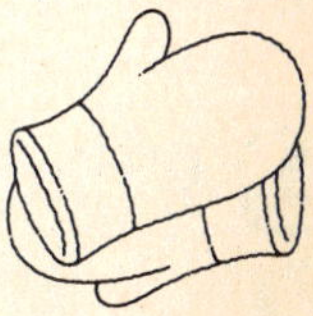
   ______________________ .

Here's what to do!

Read each shopping list. Finish each word by adding the ending **s** or **es**. Print it on the line.

Steve's List

1. 2 book______ to read
2. 3 paintbrush______
3. 6 red pencil______
4. 2 jar______ of paste

Peggy's List

1. 5 block______
2. 2 box______ of clay
3. 3 top______ to spin
4. 2 puzzle______

Pam's List

1. 8 dish______
2. 8 cup______
3. 4 glass______
4. 2 patch______ for jeans

Ron's List

1. 7 apple______
2. 5 peach______
3. 4 sandwich______
4. 2 bunch______ of grapes

Name ______________________________

Kim looked and looked for her clock.
Now she's looking for her sock.

Give this a try!

Add **ing** to each base word. Print the new word on the line.

A **base word** is a word to which the ending **ing** or **ed** can be added to form a new word.

look + **ed** = look**ed**
look + **ing** = look**ing**

1. sleep ______________
2. jump ______________
3. play ______________
4. help ______________
5. start ______________
6. work ______________
7. fish ______________
8. turn ______________

Now try this!

Add **ing** to the word beside each sentence. Print the word on the line.

9. We are ______________ for the bus. **wait**
10. Doris and Mark are ______________ rope. **jump**
11. Sam is ______________ for the bus. **look**
12. Bart's dog is ______________ with him. **stay**
13. Terry is ______________ his lunch. **hold**
14. Meg is ______________ a book. **read**
15. Now the bus is ______________ our corner! **turn**

Do it this way!

Add **ed** to each base word. Print the new word on the line. Use the new words to finish the sentences.

1 look ______ 2 want ______ 3 help ______

4 leap ______ 5 fix ______ 6 paint ______

7 Jess ______ me catch a frog.

8 We ______ a frog for a pet.

9 We ______ everywhere for frogs.

10 Suddenly a frog ______ over a rock.

11 We ______ up a box for a frog home.

Now try this!

Print each base word on the line.

12 locked ______ 13 marched ______ 14 dreamed ______

15 played ______ 16 cleaned ______ 17 passed ______

18 watched ______ 19 wanted ______ 20 missed ______

Name ______________________________

Give this a try!

Add **es** or **ed** to the base word in the box to finish each sentence. Print the word on the line.

1 The girls ____________ baseball after school.	play
2 Randy always watches and ____________ for Jean's team to win.	wish
3 The ball comes fast and ____________ past Jean's bat. Strike one!	brush
4 The pitcher throws and the ball ____________ toward the plate.	buzz
5 Jean swings as the ball ____________ by.	pass
6 This time Jean has not ____________.	miss
7 Randy ____________ up out of his seat.	jump
8 He ____________ until he was hoarse.	cheer

Now try this!

Add **s** or **es** to each base word in the box. Print the new word on the line.

see	fox	bush	patch	mail	line

9 ____________ 10 ____________

11 ____________ 12 ____________

13 ____________ 14 ____________

Here's what to do!

Circle the word that will finish each sentence. Print it on the line.

1	Dad goes ______________ in the stream in the woods.	fishing fished
2	While the time ______________, he looks around.	passes passing
3	Yesterday some quacking ducks ______________ by.	floats floated
4	Three baby ducks ______________ their mother.	followed following
5	Frogs were ______________ in and out of the water.	jumping jumps
6	They were ______________ for bugs to eat.	looking looked
7	Some birds were ______________ each other.	helped helping
8	While one ______________ the nest, the other looked for food.	watched watching
9	They ______________ to feed their hungry babies.	needs needed
10	Dad ______________ looking around as much as he likes fishing.	liking likes

Name ____________________

Do it this way!

Add **ing** to the base word in the box. Print it on the line.

When a short-vowel word ends in a single consonant, usually double the consonant before adding **ing.**
stop + ing = stopping

1. Maria and Jess were ____________________ to go shopping. **plan**

2. First they went ____________________ in the park. **jog**

3. Children were ____________________ on the swings. **swing**

4. Some horseback riders were ____________________ around. **trot**

5. Other people were ____________________ along a path. **walk**

6. They saw two bunnies ____________________ by. **hop**

7. A turtle was ____________________ at a bug. **snap**

8. A man was ____________________ hot dogs. **roast**

9. His dog was ____________________ for one. **beg**

10. "____________________ in the park was fun," said Maria. **Run**

11. "Now let's go ____________________," Jess said. **shop**

Here's what to do!

Add **ed** to the word beside each sentence to make it tell about the past. Print the word on the line.

To make a word tell about the past, usually add **ed.** If a short vowel word ends in a single consonant, usually double the consonant before adding **ed.**

I **skip** on my way home.

Yesterday I **skipped** on my way home.

1	My dog ________ his tail when I got home.	**wag**
2	He ________ up on me with a happy smile.	**hop**
3	When I ________ him, my hand got muddy.	**pat**
4	"Wags, you need to be ________!"	**scrub**
5	I ________ him up.	**pick**
6	Then I ________ him in the tub.	**dip**
7	He ________ around in the water.	**jump**
8	He ________ water everywhere!	**splash**
9	I laughed as I ________ him.	**watch**
10	When Wags ________, he was clean but I was a mess!	**stop**
11	I ________ up the mess.	**clean**
12	Then I ________ with Wags.	**play**

Name ______________________________

Here's what to do!

Circle the word that finishes each sentence. Print it on the line.

If a word ends with a silent **e**, drop the **e** before adding **ing** or **ed.**
I **bake** cookies with my mom.
We **baked** cookies yesterday.
We are **baking** cookies today, too.

1. Yesterday I ______________ to the park. — jogged / jogging

2. Then I ______________ home. — walked / walking

3. Today I am ______________ with friends. — skating / skated

4. We are ______________ for lunch. — stopped / stopping

Now do this!

Read each pair of sentences. Add **ing** or **ed** to the base word. Print the word on the line.

5. **clean** Today Dad is ______________ the garage.
   He ______________ the car yesterday.

6. **save** I am ______________ my money to buy a bike.
   Last week I ______________ almost $3.00.

7. **wag** Last night my dog was happy, so she ______________ her tail.
   She is ______________ her tail now, too.

Give this a try!

Add **ing** to each base word. Print the new word on the line.

1. ride ______
2. fry ______
3. rub ______
4. hide ______
5. frame ______
6. dig ______
7. take ______
8. jump ______
9. poke ______
10. ship ______
11. pack ______
12. quit ______

Now try this!

Add **ed** to each base word. Print the new word on the line.

13. pin ______
14. rock ______
15. chase ______
16. hop ______
17. march ______
18. bake ______
19. wish ______
20. drop ______
21. hope ______
22. quack ______

Name ______________________________

Do it this way!

Add the ending in the box to each word below it. Print the new words.

ing	ed	s or es
1 wave ________	4 skip ________	7 peach ________
2 drop ________	5 like ________	8 pass ________
3 smile ________	6 press ________	9 tree ________

Now do this!

Finish each sentence by adding the correct ending to the base word in the box. Print the new word on the line

10 I like ________ all kinds of books. **read**

11 Yesterday I ________ a good storybook at the library. **spot**

12 I also ________ out a cookbook. **check**

13 It ________ you how to cook. **teach**

14 I ________ a pie after I read it. **bake**

15 My brother is ________ his money. **save**

16 He ________ every joke book he sees. **get**

Do it this way!

Add **ed** or **ing** to the words in the box. Use the new words to finish the sentences.

bake	come
have	help
plan	cut

1. Our grandparents are ________________ over for dinner.
2. We are ________________ to have pizza and salad.
3. We ________________ the pizza first.
4. Now Carl is ________________ vegetables for the salad.
5. Lisa ________________ make the dessert.
6. We're ________________ fun!

Now do this!

Draw a box around each base word.

7. d r e s s e d
8. b u z z e s
9. c o o k e d
10. p l a y s
11. p u f f e d
12. b r u s h i n g
13. d r i v e s
14. l o a d i n g
15. b o x e s
16. d i s h e s
17. s n a p p i n g
18. p a r k i n g
19. w i s h e d
20. s t a y e d
21. s w i m m i n g

Name ______________________

Carrie is helpful around her playful baby sister.

Give this a try!

Add the ending **ful** to each base word. Print the new word on the line. Use the new words to finish the sentences.

You can make a new word by adding the ending **ful** to a base word.
help + **ful** = **helpful**

1. care ______________________
2. cheer ______________________

3. wonder ______________________
4. use ______________________

5. Pablo thought a skateboard would be very ______________________.
6. He promised to be ______________________ if he got one.
7. His family looked ______________________ when they gave him his gift.
8. It was a skateboard! What a ______________________ gift!

Now try this!

Draw a box around each base word.

9. u s e f u l
10. h o p e f u l
11. r e s t f u l
12. h a r m f u l
13. f e a r f u l
14. h e l p f u l
15. p l a y f u l
16. c a r e f u l

The owl is fearless in the darkness.

Do it this way!

Add **less** or **ness** to each base word. Print the new word on the line. Use the new words to finish the sentences.

You can add the ending **less** or **ness** to a base word to make a new word.

fear + **less** = **fearless**

dark + **ness** = **darkness**

less		ness	
1 use	__________	5 thick	__________
2 sleep	__________	6 dark	__________
3 harm	__________	7 loud	__________
4 fear	__________	8 sharp	__________

9. It is __________ to tell me the bear is harmless.

10. I am not brave and __________.

11. When I think about the bear I'm __________.

12. The bear's eyes are glowing in the __________.

13. The __________ of its snarls worries me.

14. I can almost feel the __________ of its teeth.

15. I see the __________ of its strong legs.

Name ____________________

The bunny runs quickly.

Here's what to do!

Add the ending **ly** to each base word. Print the new word on the line.

Add the ending **ly** to a base word to make a new word.
quick + **ly** = **quickly**

1. glad ____________
2. swift ____________
3. soft ____________
4. brave ____________
5. loud ____________
6. slow ____________
7. love ____________
8. near ____________

Now do this!

Circle each **ly** ending in the sentences. Print the base words on the lines.

9. Tigers walk softly. ____________
10. Lions roar bravely. ____________
11. Monkeys screech loudly. ____________
12. Turtles crawl slowly. ____________
13. Deer run swiftly. ____________
14. I watch them at the zoo gladly. ____________
15. The zoo near my house is lovely. ____________

Give this a try!

Match the base word in the first column with the new word in the second column. Print the letter on the line.

1

_____	quick	**a.** slowly
_____	sweet	**b.** quickly
_____	slow	**c.** sweetly
_____	loud	**d.** loudly
_____	nice	**e.** nicely

2

_____	glad	**a.** softly
_____	soft	**b.** nearly
_____	near	**c.** lovely
_____	love	**d.** gladly
_____	brave	**e.** bravely

3

_____	use	**a.** playful
_____	play	**b.** handful
_____	cheer	**c.** useful
_____	hand	**d.** harmful
_____	harm	**e.** cheerful

4

_____	care	**a.** fearless
_____	sleeve	**b.** helpless
_____	fear	**c.** jobless
_____	job	**d.** careless
_____	help	**e.** sleeveless

5

_____	home	**a.** sleepless
_____	sleep	**b.** cheerless
_____	use	**c.** homeless
_____	wire	**d.** useless
_____	cheer	**e.** wireless

6

_____	good	**a.** softness
_____	dark	**b.** sadness
_____	kind	**c.** darkness
_____	sad	**d.** goodness
_____	soft	**e.** kindness

Name ______________________________

Here's what to do!

Add an ending from the box to finish the word in each sentence.
Print it on the line. Trace the whole word.

ly	ful	less	ness

1. Polly was usually brave and fear______.
2. Today she was lone______ in her new school.
3. She thought of her old friends with sad______.
4. She remembered all their kind______.
5. Sudden______ she saw some girls smiling at her.
6. Now she felt more cheer______.

Now do this!

Read the words in the box. Print each word below its definition.

fearless	darkness	safely	playful

7. with no fear ______
8. full of play ______
9. in a safe way ______
10. being dark ______

Do it this way!

Add the ending in each box to the base words. Print the new words on the lines.

ly

1. quiet ______________________
2. glad ______________________

less

3. help ______________________
4. fear ______________________

ful

5. use ______________________
6. skill ______________________

ness

7. dark ______________________
8. black ______________________

Now do this!

Add an ending to the base word in the box to finish each sentence. Print the new word on the line.

9. Owls like the ______________________ of night.	dark
10. In the ______________________ they can hunt.	black
11. They are ______________________ hunters.	skill
12. Their sharp eyes are ______________________.	use
13. They fly ______________________ with no sound.	quiet
14. After a long night, owls fly ______________________ home.	safe
15. Then they ______________________ nap all day.	glad

Name ______________________________

The first dog is small,
But the next one is smaller.
Do you know which one is
smallest?

Here's what to do!

Add the ending **er** and **est** to each word.
Print the new words on the lines.

You can add the ending **er** to a base word to make a new word that tells about two things. Add the ending **est** to tell about more than two things.

small smaller smallest

	er	est
1 near	____________	____________
2 long	____________	____________
3 fast	____________	____________
4 dark	____________	____________
5 thick	____________	____________
6 deep	____________	____________
7 soft	____________	____________

Now do this!

Draw a picture to show the meaning of each word.

8 long

9 longer

10 longest

Give this a try!

Finish each sentence by adding **er** or **est** to each base word. Use **er** to tell about two things. Use **est** to tell about more than two things. Print the word on the line.

1 tall

Meg is ______________________ than Jay.

2 hard

The rock is ______________________ than the soap.

3 fast

The horse is the ______________________ of the three.

4 long

The top fish is the ______________________.

5 cold

Ice is ______________________ than water.

6 small

The ant is the ______________________.

Name ______________________

Give this a try!

Add **er** and **est** to each word. Print the new words on the lines.

When a word ends in **y** after a consonant, change the **y** to **i** before adding **er** or **est.**

busy + **est** = **busiest**

	er	est
1 silly	________	________
2 happy	________	________
3 windy	________	________
4 fluffy	________	________

Now try this!

Finish each sentence by adding **er** or **est** to the base word in the box.

5 Today was Justin's ________ kind of day. **happy**

6 He got to the bus stop ________ than he did yesterday. **early**

7 It was ________ than it had been all week. **sunny**

8 He made up the ________ joke he could. **silly**

9 The other kids said it was the ________ one they had heard. **funny**

Give this a try!

Circle the name of each picture.

When a word ends in **y** after a consonant, change the **y** to **i** before adding **es.**

story + **es** = stor**ies**

1 

daisy daisies

2 

cherry cherries

3 

lily lilies

Now do this!

Use the rule to add **es** to the word beside each sentence. Finish the sentence by printing the new word on the line.

4 We wrote ________________ for our class book. **story**

5 Mine was about my dog's new ________________ . **puppy**

6 Lily wrote about planting ________________ . **daisy**

7 Penny's story was about raising ________________ . **bunny**

8 Carol told us about picking ________________ . **cherry**

9 Marty gave ideas for birthday ________________ . **party**

10 Jerry told how to take care of ________________ . **pony**

11 Tony wrote about his collection of ________________ . **penny**

12 When we finished, we made extra ________________ . **copy**

Name ______________________________

Do it this way!

Add endings to make the words mean more than one.

1 bunny ______

2 city ______

3 box ______

4 lily ______

5 dress ______

6 pony ______

Now do this!

Circle the word that will finish each sentence. Print it on the line. Then print the name of each picture.

7 Mary's birthday ______ was fun.
(party, parties)

8 Her dad read scary ______ in the dark.
(story, stories)

9 We tried to toss ______ into bottles.
(penny, pennies)

10 Instead of cake, we ate ______ pie.
(cherry, cherries)

11 Then we got little ______ to take home.
(candy, candies)

12  ______

13  ______

14  ______

Here's what to do!

Change the **y** to **i** and add **es** to the word in each box. Print the new words to finish the sentences.

1. Farms are different from ______________________. | city
2. Sometimes my friends and our ______________________ visit a farm. | family
3. Sometimes there are lots of ______________________ in the fields. | daisy
4. Some ______________________ grow by the streams. | lily
5. We like to ride the ______________________. | pony
6. There are many different animal ______________________. | baby
7. It's fun to play with the ______________________. | bunny
8. We usually see some ______________________. | puppy
9. Fruits and ______________________ grow on farms. | berry
10. We climb trees to pick ______________________. | cherry
11. I like to write ______________________ about our trips to the country. | story
12. I give ______________________ to my friends to read. | copy

Name ______________________

Will you go sailing with me today?
The sun is shining, what do you say?

Do it this way!

Find the word in the box that names each picture. Print it on the line.

In a **vowel pair,** two vowels come together to make one long vowel sound. When a word or syllable has a vowel pair, the first vowel stands for the long sound and the second vowel is silent. You can hear the long **a** sound in **sailing** and **today.**

sail	pay	rain
tail	hay	tray
spray	chain	nail

1. 
____

2. 
____

3. 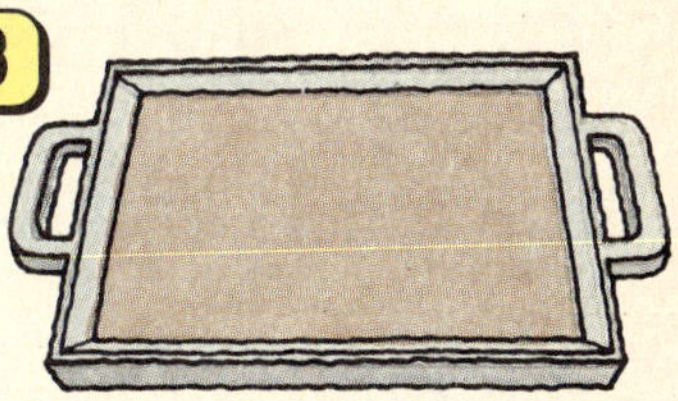
____

4. 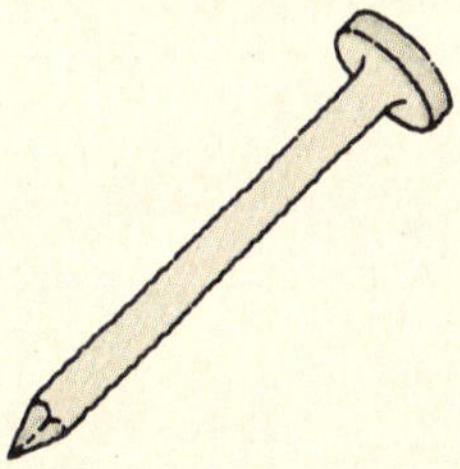
____

5. 
____

6. 
____

7. 
____

8. 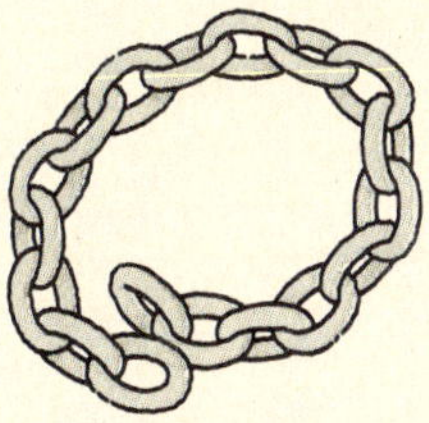
____

9. 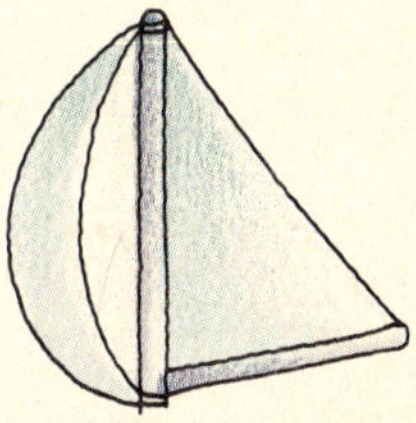
____

Here's what to do!

Find the word in the box that answers each riddle. Print it on the line.

chain	stain	mailbox	hay	pail	rain	tray
hair	paint	chair	train	gray	sail	day

1. I ride on railroad tracks. ____________
2. You put letters in me. ____________
3. I am a blend of black and white. ____________
4. If I start, you put on a raincoat. ____________
5. You can sit on me. ____________
6. I am made of many links. ____________
7. I am part of a boat. ____________
8. I am an ink spot on a shirt. ____________
9. I am piled in a stack. ____________
10. You can use a comb on me. ____________
11. You can carry water in me. ____________
12. I am spread on a wall. ____________
13. You carry food on me. ____________
14. I come before night. ____________

Name ______________________________

Do it this way!

Circle the name of each picture.

Vowel pairs **ee** and **ea** can make the long **e** sound. You can hear the long **e** sound in **jeep** and **seal.**

1

sell
seal
seed

2

jeep
jeans
peep

3

bean
bed
bee

4

leaf
lean
leak

5

jeeps
jeans
jets

6

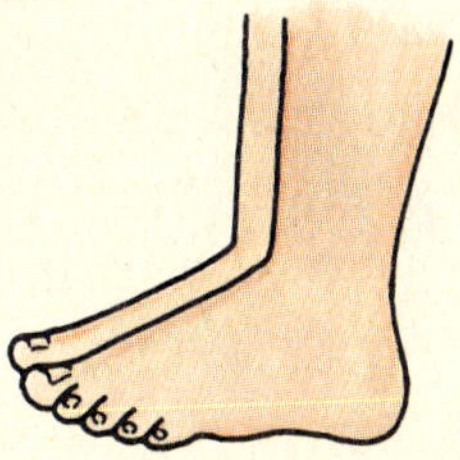

feed
feet
feel

7

deep
deeds
deer

8

meat
met
team

9

eat
each
ear

10

peach
peace
pear

11

seal
seed
send

12

team
test
teeth

Here's what to do!

Find the word in the box that will finish each sentence. Print it on the line. Then print the two vowels that stand for its long **e** sound.

keep	eager	easy	meal	feet	steer
beaver	each	teeth	leaves	seem	seen

1. Have you ever ______________ a beaver? ______
2. A ______________ likes to chew down trees. ______
3. It makes a ______________ of the bark. ______
4. It drags ______________ branch home to build a dam. ______
5. It only ______________ the stump behind. ______
6. A beaver's ______________ have to be strong. ______
7. Its webbed ______________ help it swim along. ______
8. It uses its tail to ______________ . ______
9. It's not ______________ being a beaver. ______
10. Beavers always ______________ to be working. ______
11. They ______________ working until all their work is done. ______
12. That's why busy people are often called "______________ beavers." ______

8 What is your favorite game to play? Draw a picture and write a sentence telling about it.

Hide and Seek

This book belongs to

________________. 1

"I wish Ray would find me," thought Jean.
6 "I'm getting tired of waiting."

"Don't peek!" yelled Jean as she ran to find a hiding place.
"No way!" said Ray. He leaned against a tree and counted, "One, two, three . . ." 3

"Hi, Ray," said Jean, "Do you want to play on the train today?"
"No, I like playing hide and seek best," said Ray.
"Okay," said Jean. "You're it!"

2

FOLD

Just then Jean took a peek.
She didn't see Ray anywhere.
Suddenly, she felt a tap on her shoulder. "You're it!" yelled Ray as he laughed and ran off to hide.

7

"If I hide in the train he's sure to see me," thought Jean. "I know, I'll hide behind this tree."

4

FOLD

The tree hid Jean so well, she couldn't see Ray.
She didn't hear Ray say, "Here I come."
"This sure is a neat hiding place," thought Jean.

5

Name ____________________

Do it this way!

Circle the word that will finish each sentence. Print it on the line.

The vowel pair **ie** sometimes has the long **i** sound. You can hear the long **i** sound in **tie.** The vowel pair **oe** has the long **o** sound. You can hear the long **o** sound in **hoe.**

1		My dad, ________, and I went to the store.	jay Joe jot
2		Along the way, we saw a ________ by the road.	die doe day
3	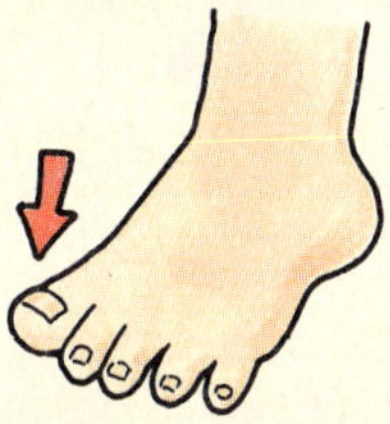	When we got there, Joe stubbed his ________.	tie toe lie
4		My dad needed to buy a new ________.	hoe hay hit
5	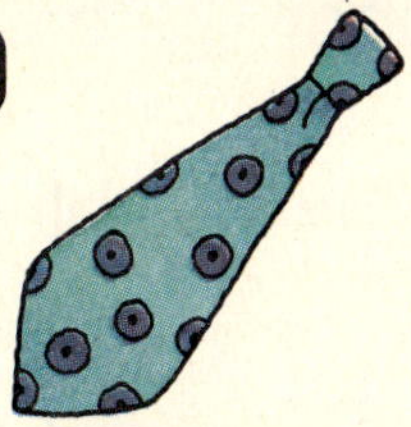	I wanted to buy a new red ________.	tie toe lie
6		We all had some ________ when we got home.	pie pine pile

Give this a try!

Print the name for each picture on the line below it.

The vowel pair **ow** sometimes has the long **o** sound. The vowel pair **oa** has the long **o** sound. You can hear the long **o** sound in **bowl** and **boat.**

boat	rainbow	goat	bow	soap	bowl

1  ____________

2  ____________

3  ____________

4  ____________

5 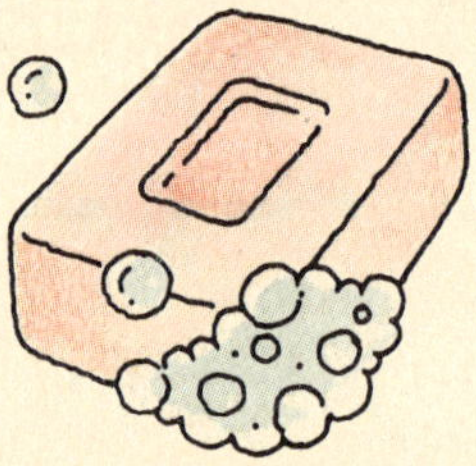 ____________

6  ____________

Now try this!

Circle the word that will finish each sentence. Print it on the line.

7 Isn't it fun to ride in a ____________? boot boat

8 Sailboats move when the wind ____________. blows blues

9 You use oars to ____________ some boats. raw row

10 Tugboats ____________ other boats along. tow too

11 Steamboats use steam to ____________ along the river. float floor

Name ______________________________

Do it this way!

Find the word in the box that will finish each sentence. Print it on the line. Then circle the two vowels in the word that stand for the long vowel sound.

day
loads
paint
peach
pie
sheep
hoes

1. Farmer Gray shears his ______________ .
2. He ______________ the wool into his truck.
3. Then he ______________ weeds in the garden.
4. Farmer Gray picks a ripe ______________ for a snack.
5. He will pick a few more to make a ______________ .
6. Then he will put a new coat of ______________ on the shed.
7. He is ready to sleep at the end of the ______________ .

Now do this!

Make a word that answers each riddle by adding beginning and ending consonants.

8. It is something warm to wear. ___oa___
9. A dog wags it. ___ai___
10. They need socks. ___ee___
11. Seven of them make a week. ___ay___
12. You have five of these on each foot. ___oe___
13. You can wear these around your neck. ___ie___

Here's what to do!

Find the name of each picture in the box. Print it on the line.

hoe	pie	hay	tree	jeans	boat	bowl	daisy

1  ____________

2 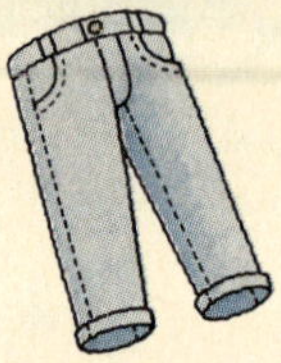 ____________

3  ____________

4  ____________

5  ____________

6  ____________

7  ____________

8  ____________

Now do this!

Find a vowel pair in the box that will finish the word in each sentence. Print it on the line. Trace the whole word.

ai
ay
ee
ea
ie
oa
oe
ow

9 Joe had a very bad ____d____.

10 Nothing s____med to go right.

11 First the hose sprang a l____k.

12 Water began to fl____ all over.

13 Then Joe got s____ked.

14 Have you ever had a day like J____ did?

Paste your baby picture inside this picture frame.
Write one or two sentences telling what you were like as a baby.

8

My, You've Grown!

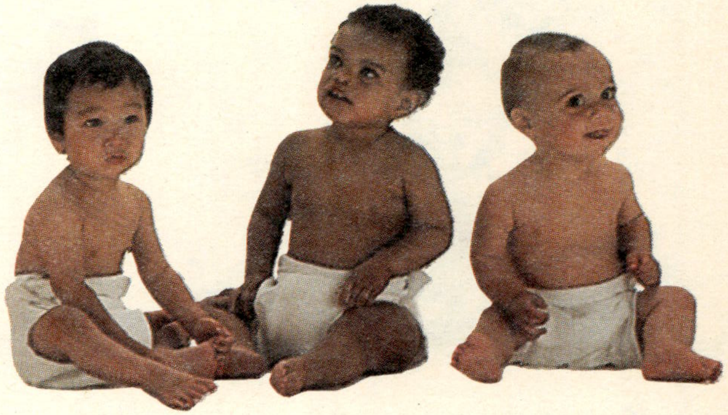

This book belongs to

________________________.

1

FOLD

A baby deer is called a fawn. Its mother is called a doe.
The mother protects her fawn from danger.

6

A baby horse, called a foal, tries to walk the day it's born.
At first, it won't roam far from its mother.
Later, the foal goes to find oats on its own.

3

FOLD

You've grown a lot from head to toe since you were born!
All animals grow and change as they get older.

2

A baby dragonfly begins life underwater. When its outer skin splits open, it flies off into the sky!

7

FOLD

A baby goat is called a kid. When it's full grown, it will have hollow horns and a beard.

4

A toad begins its life as an egg. Then it changes into a tadpole and finally into a toad.

5

FOLD

Name ______________________________

Look for me in the forest or in the zoo.
I have long fur, stripes, and a mask, too.
What am I?

Here's what to do!

Circle the word that will finish each sentence. Print it on the line.

In a **vowel digraph,** two vowels together can make a long or a short sound, or have a special sound all their own. You can hear the different sounds of the vowel digraph **oo** in **look** and **zoo.**

1. I felt something ______________ in my mouth.	broom loose
2. Was it a ______________?	tool tooth
3. I ran to my ______________.	room zoo
4. I stood on a ______________ to look in the mirror.	spoon stool
5. My tooth should fall out ______________.	moon soon
6. At ______________ it was time for lunch.	soon noon
7. I took a bite of ______________ with my spoon.	food fool
8. Out came my loose tooth on the ______________.	soothe spoon
9. My friend lost a tooth, ______________.	too zoo

Answer: A raccoon.

Here's what to do!

Find a word in the box that will finish each sentence. Print it on the line.

cookie
book
look
cook
good
took
stood
hook

1. I was looking for a good ______________.
2. I took a ______________ at a cookbook.
3. I ______________ in line to pay for the book.
4. Then I ______________ my new book home.
5. I decided to ______________ something.
6. I took my apron off a ______________ and put it on.
7. I tried a ______________ recipe.
8. The cookies were very ______________.

Now do this!

Print the missing letters of each picture's name. Print the missing letters for a word that rhymes with it. Trace the whole word.

9.

b______

sh______

10.

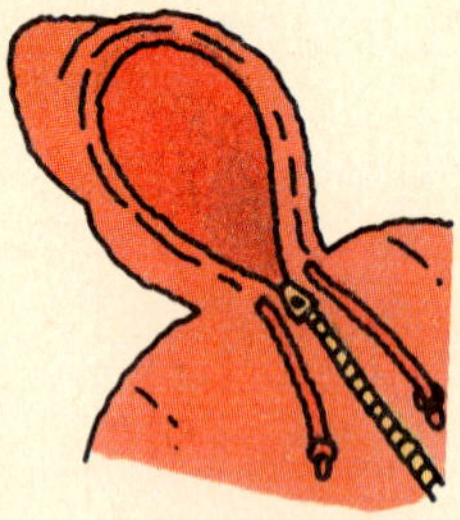

h______

st______

11.

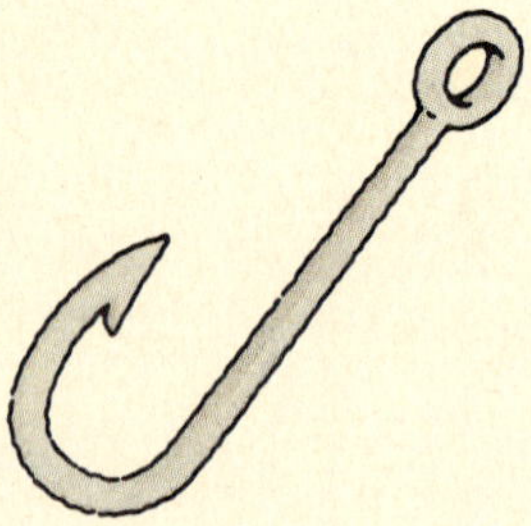

h______

br______

12.

w______

g______

Name ______________________________

Here's what to do!

Find the word in the box that will finish each sentence. Print it on the line.

The vowel digraph **ea** can stand for the short **e** sound. You can hear the short **e** sound in **ready.**

ahead
already
breakfast
spread
bread
breath
head

1. When you wake up, take a deep ______________ .
2. It will help clear your ______________ .
3. Now you are ready for ______________ .
4. Here is some ______________ to make toast.
5. You can ______________ butter and jam on it.
6. The eggs are ______________ made.
7. Go ______________ and eat.

Now do this!

Circle the correct word to finish each sentence.

8. What is the (feather, weather, leather) like today?
9. Will you need to wear a (sweater, weather, meadow)?
10. Maybe you will need a (ready, heavy, cleanser) coat.
11. Is it cold enough for (bread, thread, leather) boots?
12. Cover your (head, heavy, breakfast) with a warm hat.
13. Now you are (meadow, heavy, ready) to go outside.

Do it this way!

Say the name of each picture. Circle the words with the same **ea** sound as the picture's name.

1

seat
bread
meat
bean

2
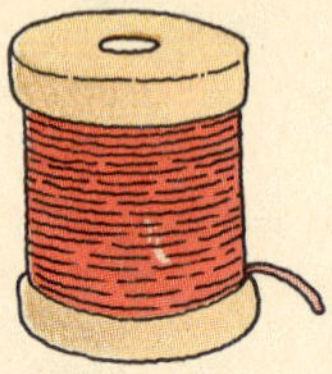
bread
beach
heavy
treat

3
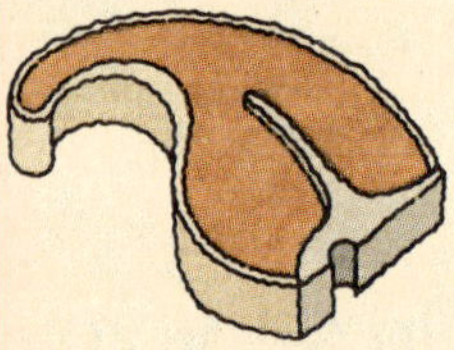
reach
steam
break
great

4

dream
mean
beak
health

5

head
heavy
lean
steak

6

steak
tea
teacher
great

7

beaver
team
leather
beans

8

bread
weather
seal
leather

9

ready
heavy
bread
bean

10

beach
teach
health
reach

11
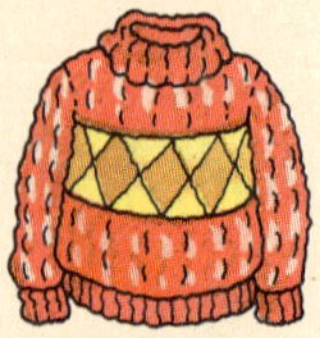
break
leather
thread
weather

12

meat
great
heat
leak

Name ______________________________

Here's what to do!

Find the word in the box that will finish each sentence. Print it on the line.

The vowel digraphs **au** and **aw** usually have the same sound. You can hear the sound of **au** and **aw** in **August** and **paw.**

drawing
autumn
straws
haul
August
lawn
pause
yawn
crawls
Paula

1. ______________ is a lazy month.
2. We ______________ in our work to relax.
3. ______________ and I play games in the shade.
4. I water the ______________ in the evenings.
5. We ______________ the picnic basket to the lake.
6. After swimming, we ______________ and nap in the sun.
7. We sip lemonade through ______________.
8. My baby brother ______________ on the beach.
9. Summer's end is ______________ near.
10. Soon ______________ will come and school will start.

Here's what to do!

Find a word in a crayon that will finish each sentence. Print it on the line.

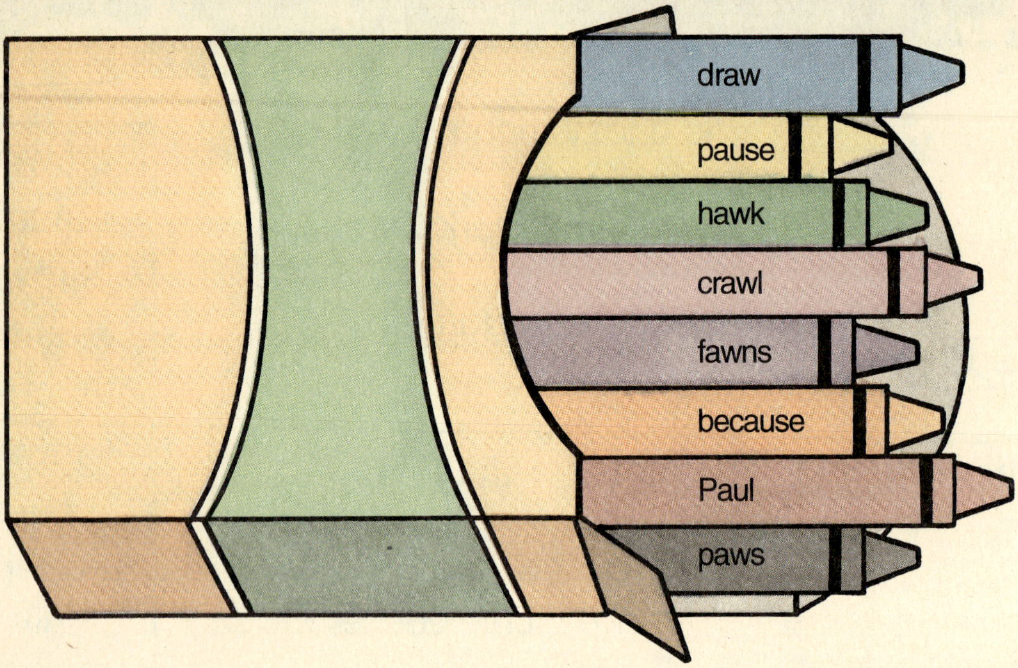

1. ______________ likes to draw.
2. He draws and draws without a ______________.
3. He can ______________ animals that look real.
4. Paul can make a ______________ that has sharp claws.
5. His turtles almost seem to ______________.
6. He draws dogs with huge ______________.
7. He draws ______________ hiding in trees.
8. Paul draws so well ______________ he practices a lot.

Name ____

Here's what to do!

Say the name of the first picture in each row. Fill in the bubble below the picture with the same vowel sound.

1
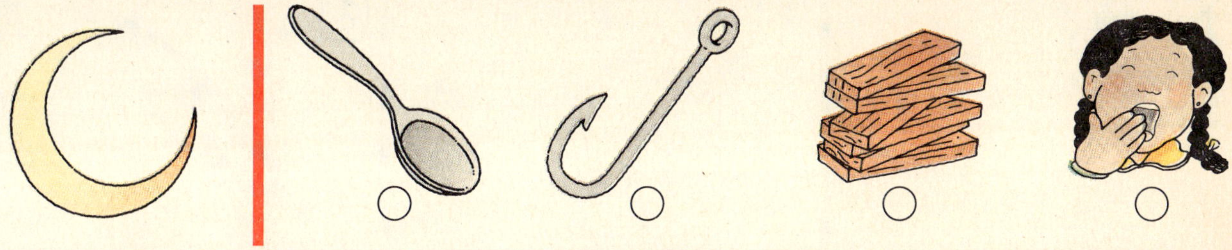

2

3

4
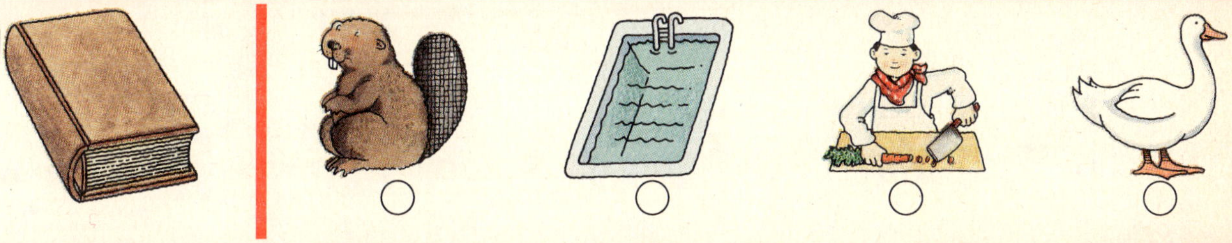

5
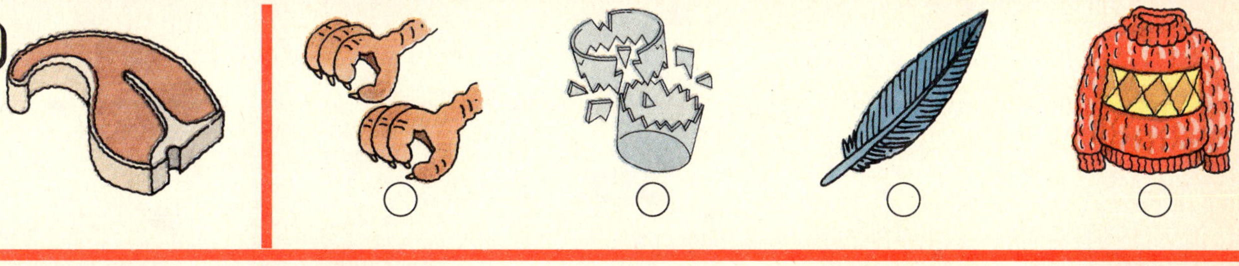

6
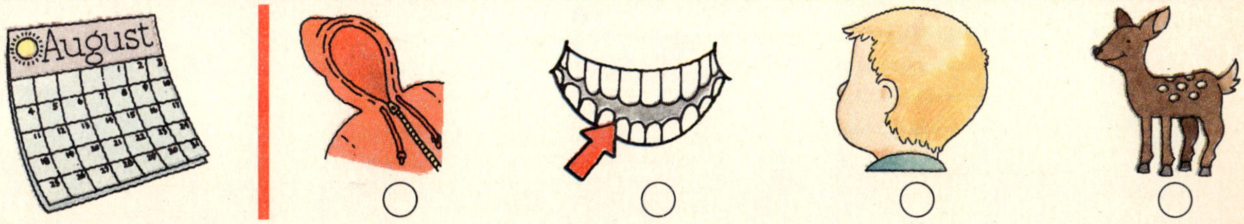

Here's what to do!

Say the name of each picture. Circle the letters that stand for the vowel sound in the picture's name. Then print the letters to finish its name. Trace the whole word.

1. 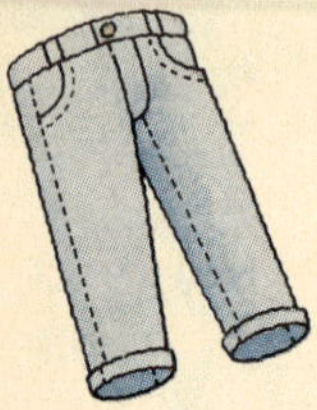
aw / ea / oo
j ___ ns

2. 
aw / ea / oo
br ___ d

3. 
aw / oo / ea
f ___ ther

4. 
ea / au / oo
sp ___ n

5. 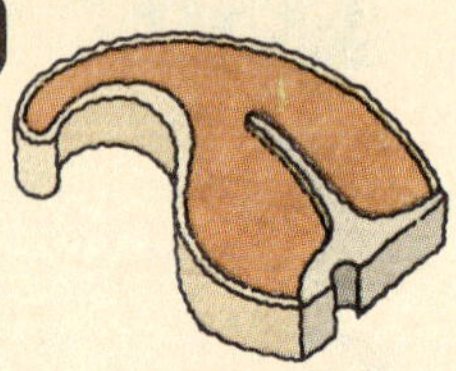
oo / ea / aw
st ___ k

6. 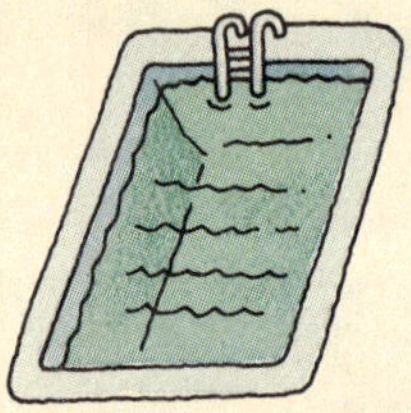
au / ea / oo
p ___ l

7. 
oo / au / ea
w ___ d

8. 
aw / oo / ea
str ___

9. 
ea / aw / oo
f ___ n

10. 
aw / oo / ea
s ___

11. 
ea / oo / au
l ___ ndry

12. 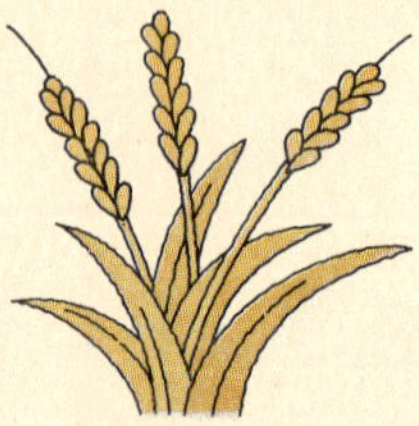
oo / ea / aw
wh ___ t

Name ______________________________

Do it this way!

The answer to each riddle rhymes with the picture name. Find the answer in the box. Print it on the line.

toe gray pie boat spoon bread hook saw

1 It rhymes with **book.**
You hang a coat on it.
What is it?

____

2 It rhymes with **paw.**
You cut wood with it.
What is it?

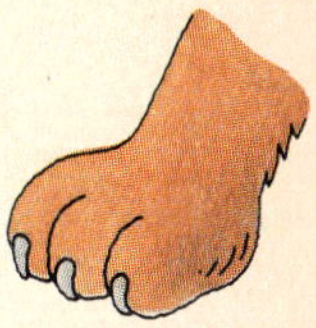

____

3 It rhymes with **doe.**
You have it on your foot.
What is it?

____

4 It rhymes with **head.**
You can eat it.
What is it?

____

5 It rhymes with **goat.**
You can row it.
What is it?

____

6 It rhymes with **tie.**
Be sure to bake it.
What is it?

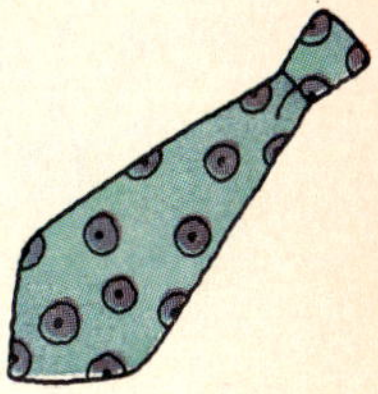

____

7 It rhymes with **moon.**
You eat with it.
What is it?

____

8 It rhymes with **hay.**
It names a color.
What is it?

____

Here's what to do!

Circle the word that will finish each sentence.

1. A baby deer is called a (seal, fawn, feather).
2. A low seat is called a (stool, school, steam).
3. A deep dish is called a (bean, book, bowl).
4. A dish under a cup is called a (saucer, saw, stool).
5. A crust filled with fruit is called a (pail, pea, pie).
6. A sharp tool to cut wood is called a (seam, saw, say).
7. A person who makes meals is called a (cook, shop, whale).
8. A kind of meat is called a (steam, steak, stoop).
9. A place where you swim is called a (paw, pear, pool).
10. Dried grass that horses eat is called (hay, ham, heat).

Now try this!

Print the missing letters to finish the name of each picture. Trace the whole word.

11. 
wh __ t

12. 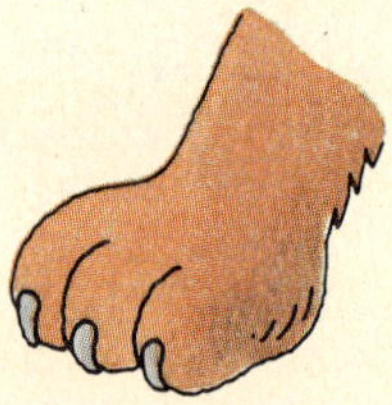
p __

13. 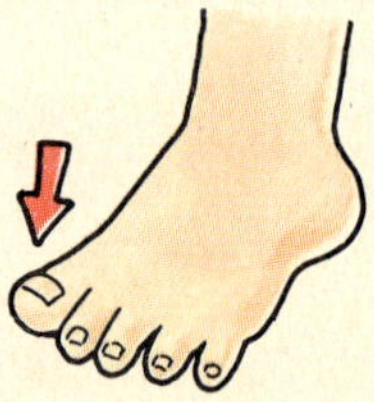
t __

14. 
j __

15. 
b __ t

16. 
tr __

17. 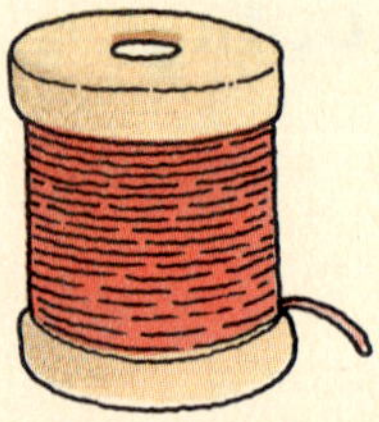
thr __ d

18. 
tr __ n

What do you think the other animals will do for the winter?
Write one or two sentences that tell what you think.

8

Autumn Is Coming

This book belongs to ____________.

1

So on this night, they pause in their work to join together and say goodbye to the warm weather for a while.

6

Moose closes his book, gets ready, and then heads for Bear's house, too.

3

Every year, on the night of the last full moon in August, Raccoon washes her paws and puts on her sweater.
Then she heads for Bear's house.

2

After the party, Bear yawns, curls up, and goes to sleep.
He dreams of the spring thaw.

7

Hawk fluffs her feathers and polishes her claws.
She too heads for Bear's house.

4

Why are the animals going to Bear's house?
Because autumn is coming.

5

FOLD

FOLD

Name ____________________

Doreen wears a round crown,
A velvet cape, and a gold gown.

Here's what to do!

Say the name of the picture. Find its name in the list. Print its letter on the line below the picture.

A **diphthong** is made up of two letters blended together to make one sound. You can hear the sound of the diphthongs **ou** and **ow** in **round** and **crown.**

1.  ____
2.  ____
3.  ____
4.  ____
5.  ____

a. clown	**j.** cow
b. cowboy	**k.** towel
c. mouse	**l.** flowers
d. shower	**m.** house
e. howl	**n.** town
f. owl	**o.** gown
g. now	**p.** pouch
h. crown	**q.** pout
cloud	mouth

6.  ____
7.  ____
8.  ____
9.  ____
10.  ____

Here's what to do!

Read each sentence. Circle the **ou** or **ow** word in the sentence. Print it on the line.

1. I live on the edge of a small town. __________
2. My house is near a farm. __________
3. I spend a lot of time outdoors. __________
4. From my yard I can see cows and horses. __________
5. In summer, I watch the farmer plow his field. __________
6. His tractor makes a loud noise. __________
7. At night, I hear many different sounds. __________
8. I can hear owls calling. __________
9. I like to watch the clouds beyond the hills. __________
10. In the fall, the flowers on the hill bloom. __________
11. Today I saw a flock of birds flying south. __________
12. They sense that winter is about to start. __________

Name ______________________________

Give this a try!

Find a word in the box that answers each riddle. Print it on the line.

owl	cow	flower	cloud	house	clown	plow	ground

1. I am in the sky.
Sometimes I bring you rain.
What am I?
____

2. I wear a funny suit.
I do many tricks.
I can make you smile.
What am I?
____

3. I am in the garden.
I am very colorful.
I may grow in your yard, too.
What am I?
____

4. You can plant seeds in me.
The farmer must plow me.
What am I?
____

5. I am wide awake in the dark.
I hoot and howl.
What am I?
____

6. You can see me at the farm.
I eat green grass.
I give you good milk.
What am I?
____

7. You can live in me.
I will keep you warm and cozy.
What am I?
____

8. The farmer uses me.
I help him make his garden.
What am I?
____

Give this a try!

Print an X beside each word in which **ow** stands for the long **o** sound.

Remember, **ow** can stand for the long **o** sound, as in **snow,** or it can make a sound of its own, as in **clown.**

1 ____ how	2 ____ snow	3 ____ own	4 ____ town
5 ____ crowd	6 ____ now	7 ____ bowl	8 ____ grow
9 ____ low	10 ____ plow	11 ____ power	12 ____ owl
13 ____ slow	14 ____ flow	15 ____ know	16 ____ show
17 ____ brown	18 ____ crow	19 ____ crown	20 ____ down
21 ____ towel	22 ____ glow	23 ____ throw	24 ____ brown
25 ____ cow	26 ____ blow	27 ____ arrow	28 ____ tower

Now try this!

Circle the **ow** word in each sentence. Print an X in the correct column to show which sound it makes.

	long vowel	**diphthong**
29 The circus came to our town.	____	____
30 We went to the show last night.	____	____
31 We sat in the very first row.	____	____
32 The star was a funny clown.	____	____
33 He made the crowd laugh.	____	____

Name ______________________________

Give this a try!

Circle the name of each picture.

The diphthongs **oi** and **oy** usually stand for the same sound. You can hear that sound in **coin** and **boy.**

1 

bow
boil
bill

2 

boy
bag
toy

3 

corn
coil
coins

4 

sail
sell
soil

5 

oak
oil
out

6 

toil
tail
toys

7 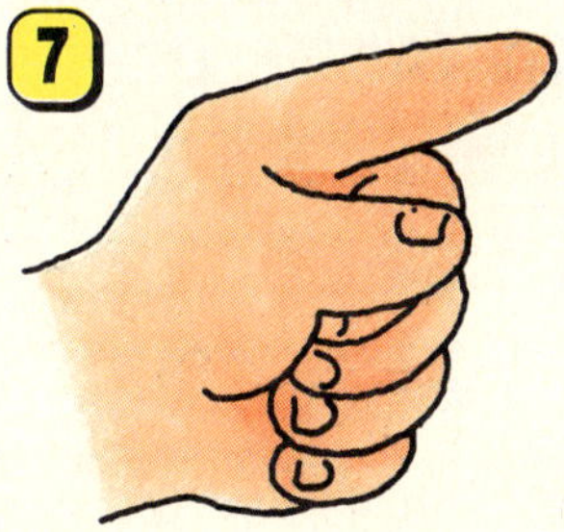

paint
point
pail

8 

noise
nail
nose

9 

fame
foil
fawn

Now try this!

Finish each sentence with a word from the box.

enjoy
toy
coins

10 I have saved a few dollars and some ______________.

11 I will buy a ______________ robot kit.

12 I will ______________ putting it together.

Here's what to do!

Read the story. Circle each **oi** word. Draw a box around each **oy** word.

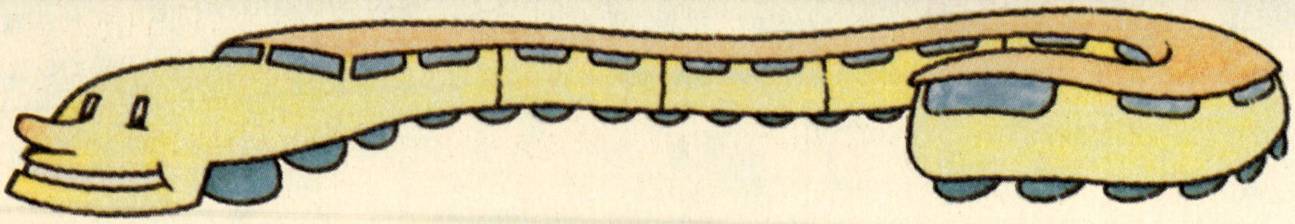

The Runaway Toy

A boy named Roy had a birthday. His grandmother and grandfather gave him a choice of toys. Roy chose a toy train. He was a very happy boy.

Roy enjoyed his toy train, but it made too much noise. Roy took out a can of oil and oiled the toy. The oil made the train less noisy. It made it go faster, too.

One day Roy oiled it too much. The train went faster and faster. It raced around the room and out the door. Roy chased it out the door and down the path. The toy train rolled up to his sister, Joy.

"Look," said Joy. "This toy wants to join me outside."

"That's my toy train," said Roy. "It ran away from me. I used too much oil."

Joy gave the toy train to Roy.

"Thank you," said Roy. "From now on I will be more careful. I will not spoil my toy with too much oil."

Now do this!

Use the words you marked to answer the questions.

1. What was the boy's name? ______________
2. What did he get for his birthday? ______________
3. What made the train go fast? ______________
4. What made Roy oil the train? ______________

Name ____________________

Do it this way!

Find the word in the box that will finish each sentence. Print it on the line.

spoil
Joy
oil
choice
joins
noise
boy
enjoy
toys
Floyd's

1. Floyd is a hungry ____________.
2. He does not want to play with his ____________.
3. Now he would ____________ a bowl of popcorn.
4. ____________ sister Joy wants popcorn, too.
5. Popcorn won't ____________ their dinner.
6. Joy ____________ Floyd in the kitchen.
7. Floyd pours some ____________ in a pan.
8. ____________ tells him to be careful.
9. The children listen for a popping ____________.
10. Did Floyd and Joy make a good ____________?

Give this a try!

Circle **yes** or **no** to answer each question.

		Yes	No
1	Is a penny a coin?	Yes	No
2	Is joy being very sad?	Yes	No
3	Can you play with a toy?	Yes	No
4	Is oil used in a car?	Yes	No
5	Is a point the same as paint?	Yes	No
6	Can you boil water?	Yes	No
7	Can you make a choice?	Yes	No
8	Is a loud noise quiet?	Yes	No

Now try this!

Find the word in the box that will finish each sentence. Print it on the line.

spoil
enjoys
toy
Joyce
noise
points
boy

9. ________ is glad the circus is in town.
10. She loves the ________ of the crowd.
11. The clown rides in a ________ car.
12. She smiles and ________ at the funny clown.
13. She sees a ________ standing up on a horse.
14. Nothing can ________ the day for Joyce.
15. Joyce always ________ a day at the circus.

Name ____________________

Here's what to do!

Find the word in the box that will finish each sentence. Print it on the line.

The diphthong **ew** stands for the long **u** sound. You can hear the long **u** sound in **new** and **few**.

grew
blew
chew
flew
new
threw
knew
few

1. I bought a ____________ pack of sugarless gum.
2. I put a ____________ pieces into my mouth.
3. I began to ____________ the gum.
4. Then I ____________ a giant bubble.
5. That bubble grew and ____________ .
6. Suddenly, I ____________ I was in trouble.
7. The bubble broke, and pieces ____________ everywhere.
8. I ____________ the pieces of chewed gum away.

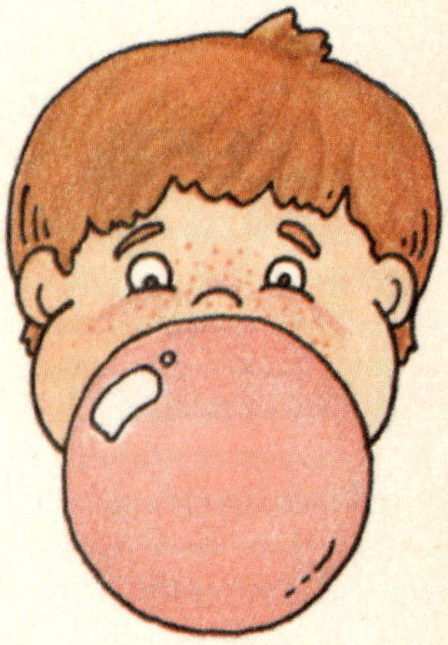

Now do this!

Print the missing letters for a word that rhymes with each word. Trace the whole word.

9. few — st____
10. crew — thr____
11. grew — fl____

Here's what to do!

Circle the word that will finish each sentence.

1. (Drew, Blew, Knew) wanted a pet.
2. He went to (Crew, Dew, Flew) the Coop Pet Shop.
3. He saw puppies (chewing, stewing, mewing) on toy bones.
4. Baby birds (flew, stew, knew) around their cage.
5. They (few, threw, grew) seeds on the floor.
6. Drew really wanted a (mew, stew, new) kitten.
7. He saw a (chew, crew, grew) of kittens.
8. A (few, threw, grew) were very cute.
9. One kitten looked at him and (flew, mewed, chewed).
10. Drew (grew, dew, knew) he wanted that kitten.

---

11. Drew named him (Mews, Stews, Dews) because he always mewed.
12. That kitten (new, grew, chew) bigger every day.
13. Mews liked it when Drew (few, threw, mew) a toy to him.
14. He liked to (chew, new, stew) on Drew's shoestrings.
15. Mew tried to hide under the (screws, grew, newspaper).
16. From the window he watched birds as they (flew, crew, dew).
17. When the wind (blew, drew, stew), Mews chased fallen leaves.
18. He licked drops of morning (mew, dew, chew).
19. Before Drew (threw, few, knew) it, Mews was his friend.
20. Drew really loved his (stew, new, flew) pet.

Name ______________________________

Give this a try!

Circle the answer to each riddle.

1. You use it when you talk.
   spoil joy soil voice

2. It means that something is wet.
   round join moist oil

3. You see them do funny tricks.
   crowns clowns browns clouds

4. You can live in it.
   house plow mouse proud

5. It is something a dog can do.
   howl coin stew new

6. Very hot water can do this.
   joy boil plow oil

7. It is something to play with.
   owl toy how crowd

8. It is something we can eat.
   mew drew stew few

9. It means "not many."
   new few dew stew

10. It means "dirt."
    soil coil boy oil

11. The farmer uses it.
    frown plow down cloud

12. A cat likes to chase it.
    house out shout mouse

Now do this!

Read the poem. Circle each **ow** word.

Chow Now?

"Moo—Moo," said Ms. Cow.
"How about some chow?
I want some now!"

"Not now, dear Ms. Cow.
Before you chow,
You help me plow!"

Do it this way!

Finish each sentence with a word that rhymes with the word in the box. Print it on the line.

1	Girls and boys can shout with ______________ .	toy
2	A shout is one sound a ______________ can make.	choice
3	Animals' voices make different ______________ .	pounds
4	Lions can roar with a powerful ______________ .	prowl
5	Wolves can ______________ at the moon.	fowl
6	A ______________ makes a little squeak.	house
7	Cows make a loud ______________ when they moo.	poise
8	These are just a ______________ voice sounds.	dew
9	______________ many others can you think of?	Now

Now do this!

Read each sentence. Circle each **oi** or **oy** word.

Troy enjoys toys.

Troy enjoys noise.

So Troy enjoys toys

That make a loud noise.

Look up at the sky.
What kind of clouds do you see?
Draw a picture of them and write a sentence that tells what they may bring.

8

All About Clouds

This book belongs to

_______________.

1

A sky like this is called a "mackerel sky."
The clouds look like fish scales.
If you see them, count on the weather changing.

6

Has it been boiling hot for days now?
If you see clouds like these, you may soon hear the noisy sound of thunder and be drowning in rain!

3

FOLD

Weather maps and clouds can tell us what the weather will be for the next few hours or days.
Here's how to tell if the weather will be enjoyable or annoying.

2

Are the clouds low in the sky?
If you live in the mountains, clouds like these may cover the ground like mist or dew.

7

FOLD

Are the clouds as gray as oysters?
Is it so dark it looks as if someone drew the curtains closed?
Snow or rain may be coming your way.

4

Warm air rises from the ground to make these clouds.
Go ahead and enjoy a picnic.
These clouds won't spoil a sunny day with rain.

5

FOLD

Name ______________________________

Today, I'll pack a snack in a paper sack.
Tomorrow, I'll repack that sack with another snack.

The prefix **re** usually means **do again.**

repack
The prefix is **re.**
The base word is **pack.**
I'll **repack** the sack.

Here's what to do!

Add **re** to the word beside each sentence. Use the new words to finish the sentences.

1 Every day I do things that I have to ______________.	do
2 When I get up, I ______________ my bed.	make
3 I ______________ my teeth after I eat.	brush
4 I ______________ my backpack before school.	pack
5 I ______________ my shoes.	tie
6 When my camera needs film, I ______________ it.	load
7 I read and ______________ my favorite books.	read
8 I write and ______________ my stories.	write
9 Every night I ______________ my alarm clock.	wind

Here's what to do!

Add **un** to the word beside each sentence. Use the new words to finish the sentences.

When the prefix **un** is added, the new word means the opposite of the original word.

Keys can **lock.** Keys can **unlock.**

unlock

The prefix is **un.**

The base word is **lock.**

1. Every day we do things and ________________ them. | do
2. We dress and ________________ . | dress
3. We button and ________________ our clothes. | button
4. We tie our shoes and then ________________ them. | tie
5. We lock and ________________ doors to go in and out. | lock
6. We buckle our seat belts and ________________ them. | buckle
7. We wrap up our lunches and then ________________ them. | wrap
8. We pack our backpacks and ________________ them. | pack
9. We load film in a camera and later ________________ it. | load
10. I am not ________________ about all this undoing. | happy
11. It just seems a little ________________ to me. | usual
12. But it's probably ________________ things will ever change. | likely

Name ______________________________

Do it this way!

Add **re** or **un** to the word beside each sentence. Use the new word to finish the sentence.

1 Last night my baby sister ________ my backpack.	packed
2 She tried to ________ my homework with her crayon.	do
3 I have to ________ my story.	write
4 Now I ________ my backpack every night.	check
5 I am very ________ about it, too.	happy
6 My things are ________ around my sister.	safe

Now do this!

Print one word that means the same as each pair of words.

7 not cooked ________

8 spell again ________

9 not safe ________

10 use again ________

11 not able ________

12 play again ________

13 not kind ________

14 tell again ________

Do it this way!

Add the prefix **un** or **re** to each underlined word. Print the new word on the line.

1. to read again

2. opposite of lock

3. to fill again

4. opposite of tie

5. opposite of buckle

6. to heat again

7. to build again

8. opposite of pack

9. to write again

10. opposite of happy

11. to play again

12. to wind again

Name ______________________________

Give this a try!

Add **dis** to each word. Use the new words to finish the sentences.

disorder
The prefix is **dis.**
The base word is **order.**

1. My dog Wags ____________ for a while.
2. Then I ____________ my shoe was missing.
3. "Why did you ____________ me Wags?"
4. "You know I'm ____________ when you take my things."
5. "That was a ____________ thing to do."
6. "Wags, you are a ____________."
7. Wags barked to ____________.
8. He pulled my shoe out of my ____________ toy chest.

appeared
covered
obey
pleased
loyal
grace
agree
orderly

Here's what to do!

Fill in the bubble beside the word that will finish each sentence. Write it on the line.

1 

Mr. Fixit will ________________________ the plug before fixing the telephone.

- ○ discolor
- ○ disconnect

2 

The rider will ________________________ and let her horse rest.

- ○ dismount
- ○ distaste

3 

Meg and Peg are twin sisters, but they ________________________ on many things.

- ○ disagree
- ○ disappear

4 

The puppy ________________________ its owner and ran outside with her hat.

- ○ dishonest
- ○ disobeyed

5 

Will loves green beans, but he ________________________ eggplant.

- ○ dislikes
- ○ disgrace

6 

Kirk made the dirt appear, so he had to make it ________________________.

- ○ disappear
- ○ distrust

Name ______________________________

Here's what to do!

Add **un, dis,** or **re** to each base word to make a new word. Print it on the line.

un or **dis**			**re** or **dis**		
1 ______ agree	2 ______ happy		7 ______ able	8 ______ writes	
3 ______ obey	4 ______ easy		9 ______ add	10 ______ like	
5 ______ lucky	6 ______ please		11 ______ pay	12 ______ loyal	

Now do this!

Add **un, dis,** or **re** to each underlined word to change the meaning of the sentence. Print the new word on the line.

13. Grandpa was <u>pleased</u> about the plans for his party. ______________________

14. He said he felt <u>easy</u> about getting gifts. ______________________

15. Sadly Sue <u>wrapped</u> the present she had made. ______________________

16. Then Jake said they would <u>obey</u> Grandpa just once. ______________________

17. With a grin, Sue <u>wrapped</u> the gift. ______________________

18. She <u>tied</u> the bow. ______________________

19. Grandpa was not <u>happy</u> with his party after all. ______________________

Do it this way!

Circle the prefix that makes sense in the sentence. Write the prefix on the line.

1. I stopped to ________load my camera at the zoo. dis re
2. I ________placed it in my camera bag. re un
3. I ________covered a large rhino looking at me. re dis
4. It seemed to be friendly, but I felt ________easy. un dis
5. I was ________sure what it might do. dis un
6. I know that may be ________fair. re un
7. I don't mean to make the rhino ________happy. un re
8. I'm not trying to be ________kind. re un
9. It's just that I ________trust huge animals. dis un
10. It would be ________honest to say it didn't scare me. re dis
11. A rhino could ________able me with its huge horn. un dis
12. I ________agree with people who say a rhino is harmless. dis re
13. That huge beast looks really ________safe to me. re un
14. I hope they remembered to ________check the lock. re dis
15. I know I would ________like seeing a rhino out of its cage. un dis
16. I wish I had ________read my books about rhinos. re dis

Name ______________________________

I see a large, white cloud in the sky.
It looks so big floating way up high.

Do it this way!

Print each word from the box beside a word that means the same thing.

Synonyms are words that have the same or almost the same meaning. **Large** and **big** mean the same thing.

glad	ill	damp	fast	little	large

1. big ______________ 2. small ______________
3. happy ______________ 4. quick ______________
5. sick ______________ 6. wet ______________

Now do this!

Circle the word in each row that means almost the same thing as the first word.

7. **jolly**	sad	big	happy	jump
8. **junk**	gems	trash	list	top
9. **pile**	heap	near	rest	stop
10. **sleep**	awake	nap	paint	read
11. **sick**	ill	quick	lazy	glad
12. **quick**	step	slow	pony	fast
13. **sound**	sad	noise	find	happy
14. **large**	huge	many	tiny	blue
15. **close**	move	let	shut	see

Do it this way!

Finish Peggy's letter. Print a word from the box that means the same thing as the word below each line.

friend	gifts	noise	fast	hope	kind	laugh
happy	races	easy	big	little	enjoy	

Dear Pablo,

I'm ____________ that you came to my party. It was
(glad)

____________ of you to bring ____________. The
(nice) (presents)

____________ book looks ____________ to read. I will
(large) (simple)

____________ reading it. When I wind up the
(like)

____________ robot, it ____________ ____________
(small) (runs) (quickly)

and makes a funny ____________. It makes me
(sound)

____________ to watch it. Thank you very much. I
(giggle)

____________ to see you soon.
(wish)

Your ____________,
(pal)

Peggy

Name ______________________________

I have a cute little dog named Paul.
His ears are big and his nose is small.

Here's what to do!

Find a word in the box that means the opposite of each word. Print its letter on the line.

Antonyms are words that are opposite or almost opposite in meaning. **Big** and **small** mean the opposite of each other.

a. old	**b.** wet	**c.** start	**d.** full	**e.** slow
f. last	**g.** down	**h.** hot	**i.** good	**j.** short
k. out	**l.** well	**m.** few	**n.** winter	**o.** long
p. far	**q.** lower	**r.** shallow	**s.** shut	**t.** awake
u. thick	**v.** fat	**w.** white	**x.** hard	

1 ____ dry	2 ____ up	3 ____ summer	4 ____ short
5 ____ near	6 ____ fast	7 ____ tall	8 ____ bad
9 ____ cold	10 ____ thin	11 ____ sick	12 ____ many
13 ____ stop	14 ____ upper	15 ____ first	16 ____ deep
17 ____ new	18 ____ empty	19 ____ open	20 ____ in
21 ____ asleep	22 ____ easy	23 ____ black	24 ____ skinny

Do it this way!

Print a word from the box that means the opposite of each word.

stop	open	full	ill	cry	night
float	hot	strong	asleep	sit	smile

1 awake

______

2 closed

______

3 empty

______

4 cold

______

5 healthy

______

6 stand

______

7 weak

______

8 sink

______

9 day

______

10 laugh

______

11 frown

______

12 go

______

Name ______________________________

What do you say to a knight before he goes to bed?

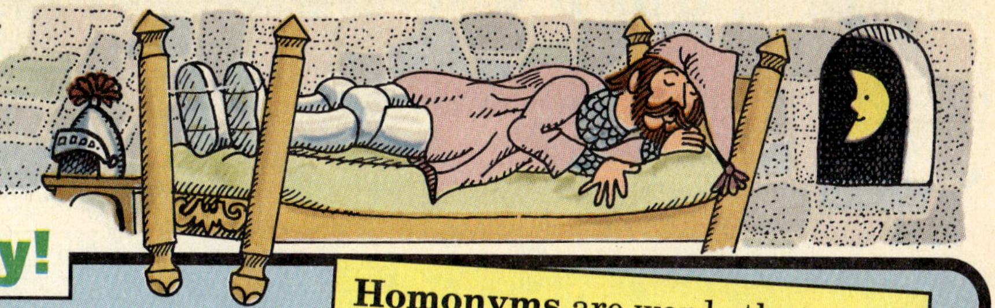

Give this a try!

Find a word in the box that sounds the same as each word below. Print it on the line.

Homonyms are words that sound alike but have different spellings and meanings. **Knight** and **night** are homonyms.

tail	here	to	road	pail	heal
blue	week	cent	sail	maid	sea

1. heel ____________
2. see ____________
3. rode ____________
4. sent ____________
5. tale ____________
6. blew ____________
7. weak ____________
8. pale ____________
9. hear ____________
10. two ____________
11. sale ____________
12. made ____________

Now try this!

Circle the word that will finish each sentence. Print it on the line.

13. Maggie ____________ her horse into the woods. road rode
14. Her puppy wagged its ____________ and ran along. tail tale
15. They saw a ____________ that hid behind a tree. dear deer
16. Maggie watched the ____________ set in the West. son sun

Answer: Night, knight!

Give this a try!

Find a word in the box that sounds the same as each word below. Print it on the line.

son	meat	blew	to	pane	tow	tale	week
heel	wait	beet	cent	sea	dear	sew	

1. weight ____________
2. sun ____________
3. weak ____________
4. sent ____________
5. blue ____________
6. beat ____________
7. deer ____________
8. two ____________
9. heal ____________
10. pain ____________
11. see ____________
12. meet ____________
13. so ____________
14. tail ____________
15. toe ____________

Now try this!

Use words from the box and the activity above to finish the sentences.

16. It had rained all ____________.
17. When Pete woke up, the ____________ was shining.
18. He could ____________ his friends playing outside.
19. He pulled on his ____________ jeans in a hurry.
20. After breakfast, he ran out ____________ play.

Name ____________________

Give this a try!

Print **S** on the line between words that mean the same thing. Print **O** on the line between words that mean the opposite.

1. first ____ last
2. little ____ small
3. under ____ over
4. hard ____ soft
5. like ____ enjoy
6. stop ____ go
7. creep ____ crawl
8. bad ____ good
9. big ____ large
10. pretty ____ ugly
11. bug ____ insect
12. float ____ sink
13. loud ____ noisy
14. present ____ gift
15. day ____ night

Now try this!

Find the word that sounds like each word. Print its number on the line.

16.
maid ____ 1. sun
son ____ 2. seem
seam ____ 3. made

17.
week ____ 1. tail
pail ____ 2. pale
tale ____ 3. weak

18.
pair ____ 1. sea
see ____ 2. pear
beet ____ 3. beat

19.
pain ____ 1. pane
blew ____ 2. in
inn ____ 3. blue

20.
deer ____ 1. two
too ____ 2. heel
heal ____ 3. dear

21.
rode ____ 1. ring
here ____ 2. road
wring ____ 3. hear

Here's what to do!

Circle two words in each box that mean the same thing.

1 cold cool seed shook	2 hair small little home	3 fast fell quick queen
4 three tree shut close	5 jump leap drink drop	6 sick snow ill blow

Now do this!

Circle two words in each box that mean the opposite.

7 little puppy jelly big	8 fly old new penny	9 bad candy rich good
10 they fast play slow	11 from dirty clean funny	12 asleep play baby awake

Now try this!

Circle the word that will finish each sentence. Print it on the line.

13 The ______________ was shining bright. sun son

14 I put on my ______________ shorts and blue hat. read red

15 I went for a sail on the ______________ . see sea

16 The wind blew the ______________ . sails sales

17 It almost ______________ my hat off, too. blew blue

18 I had a ______________ time! grate great